MW00889490

SOCIAL MEDIA MARKETING SERIES

TIKTOK MARKETING

A GUIDE TO TIKTOK ADVERTISING, GROWING YOUR FOLLOWING, BUILDING YOUR BRAND AND MAKING MONEY AS A TIKTOK INFLUENCER

MAX GOODWIN

TABLE OF CONTENTS

INTRODUCTION TO TIKTOK

What is TikTok?

TikTok is a social networking site that focuses on short videos. It was formerly known as Musical.ly and is owned by ByteDance. It serves as a platform for brand expression and brand awareness for brands, creators, and influencers. As a consequence of this, it has become a well-liked platform for both influencer marketing and the social media marketing of brands.

While TikTok shares many parallels with popular platforms such as Twitter and Instagram, it is not the same as your typical social media network. TikTok is different from other platforms because it has its own discovery algorithm. This means that every video has the same chance of going viral, no matter how popular the content creator is. This makes it possible to quickly expand a social media presence, grow quickly, and try out almost any kind of marketing strategy.

TikTok utilizes an algorithm to choose what appears in users' feeds. Every video has a legitimate potential of going viral, thanks to the algorithm's secret discovery process.

During the COVID-19 pandemic, the short-form video app grew quickly because many users had time to explore the platform and find new ways to connect with their online audiences. With 315 million downloads in Q1 2020, TikTok broke the record for the most downloads of a social app in a single quarter. This was due to its rapid growth.

One billion users are active on TikTok worldwide. In terms of social networking sites, TikTok is now ranked seventh, ahead of LinkedIn, Twitter, Pinterest, and Snapchat (excluding the Chinese counterpart Douyin, which has 600 million members).

To put this into perspective, it took Instagram six years from the time it was launched until it reached the same number of monthly active users as TikTok did in under three years. And it took Facebook the better part of four years to reach the same number of monthly active users.

TikTok is a popular social media platform because it reflects a growing trend among young people to express themselves creatively and collaborate. Users spend an average of 52 minutes each day using the app, thanks to its fast-paced nature, which keeps them interested in comparatively extended periods of time.

Ninety percent of people who use TikTok do so every day. Not only that, but they are very active on the app. It was found that 68% of people who use the social media platform TikTok view other people's videos, while 55% of those who use TikTok upload their own (Globalwebindex, 2019).

Is TikTok going to go away tomorrow?

New apps are constantly being released. Should we be concerned about TikTok? Most likely, yeah. While you never know, the app is now growing at a rapid pace. TikTok has now received over a billion downloads. In 2018, there were 663 million downloads. If you compare it to its closest competitor, Instagram, you'll see that only 444 million new people downloaded Instagram in 2018.

As of now, it has more active monthly users than any of the other social media platforms: Twitter, LinkedIn, Pinterest, and Snapchat.

What is TikTok Known for?

TikTok describes itself as a "place for short-form mobile videos." Users can make and post videos that include music, filters, and editing effects or show the person lip-syncing or dancing to a song. Videos are typically 15 seconds long; however, TikTok has gradually extended the duration offered, enabling for 10 minutes as of March 2022.

Its fast-paced video style isn't just for dance competitions and lip-synching, but that's what it's become famous for. Creators on TikTok use the site to talk about hard topics, push for change, and teach their audiences about everything from healthcare to accounting.

What is TikTok used for?

The two most popular hashtags on TikTok, #entertainment and #dance, show that it has become a key place to go for entertaining content.

Pranks, fitness, home improvement, do-it-yourself projects, beauty and skincare, fashion, recipes and cuisine, life hacks, guidance, and pets are some of the other extremely popular categories on the app.

TikTok's platform is witnessing an ever-expanding spectrum of topics addressed and covered, including more intimate and serious topics such as the following:

- Wellness tips: Medical professionals Lora Shahine and Dr. David Puder have amassed tens of thousands of fans thanks to their work in the field of reproductive health.
- The site has witnessed a rise in the popularity of at-home activities such as gardening and cooking; one example of this trend is Garden Marcus in Texas, which has more than 650 thousand followers.
- Sharing information about crimes, like when the murder victim Gabbie Petito's car was found because TikTokers had videoed it, or when a Kentucky girl was saved from an abductor because she had learned a distress hand signal from TikTok.
- As with any social platform, there can be bad things going on, like the #couchboy hashtag trend, which was used to talk about how a girlfriend surprised her boyfriend in college and how he didn't react much to it.

Content that gives users both inspiration and authenticity tends to do well. This is a growing trend for brands on social media. Many TikTok users like to see real and raw angles, which is different from Instagram, where most videos and photos have become more polished and, some might say, less real.

TikTok has started its own #LearnonTikTok campaign, which organizes educational content into categories ranging from "life hacks to scientific courses, cosmetics masterclasses, and motivational tips, to quick recipes."

This hashtag has been viewed more than 198 billion times as of December 2021 and features articles from the BBC, Cambridge University, and Cosmopolitan Magazine.

How does TikTok work?

TikTok users can find videos by using hashtags and a special algorithm. When a user logs into the app, they see a specially tailored home feed called the For You page. This is the best location to look for new and people to follow.

TikTok displays content that it believes is relevant to each individual user based on signals detected by its algorithm. The algorithm takes into account factors such as:

- Your personal preferences; country, language, and device
- Hashtags, descriptions, audio, and genre metadata for videos

- User interactions, such as the kinds of videos you watch, the accounts you follow, and the people you talk to.

Because the platform chooses content that it believes will be both intriguing and highly engaging for each individual user and posts that content within the For You tab, there is a considerable probability that content uploaded to TikTok will end up going viral on the platform. Due to how easy it is to obtain exposure through the use of a popular hashtag or a trendy sound, challenges, pranks, and dance moves spread like quickly throughout the app.

Who uses TikTok?

TikTok is most popular among teens around the world, who are typically the first to use new social media sites. They learned how to utilize the platform early on and adapted it to their preferences and requirements; as a result, many of them have amassed thousands of followers over the course of the previous several years.

Millennials and Baby Boomers who join the platform may make fun of themselves, either through their ineptitude with the app or by the content they create. Many say that their teenage family members told them to use the app or gave them ideas about how to use it.

For instance, celebrity chef Gordon Ramsey has garnered over 28.9 million followers on TikTok (as of November 2021) after his Gen Z-aged daughter, Tilly, helped him learn how to utilize the platform for dance challenges.

In spite of its popularity among younger generations, TikTok appears to be retaining its older users.

TikTok is currently accessible in 154 countries around the world. According to 2019 Global Web Index data, TikTok penetration appears to be highest in Asia, where more than one-third of users aged 16-64 had an account. The rest of the world is pretty close, with 12 percent penetration in North America and 10 percent penetration everywhere else (Latin America and Europe).

Global businesses have recognized TikTok as an important tool for engaging with youthful audiences, encouraging user-generated content and collaborating with relevant influencers. Paid advertisements, as well as campaigns run by influencers, have been spotted on the TikTok app by brands such as Nike, Skittles, Fenty Beauty, Pepsi, Calvin Klein, Sony, and FIFA, to name a few. If you're a brand that wants to connect with TikTok creators, you can use a tracker tool to find the right people to talk to.

Celebrities like Reese Witherspoon, Snoop Dogg, Dua Lipa, and Kendall Jenner have been using TikTok a lot more, especially in 2020 when the COVID pandemic was happening and they were looking for ways to stay relevant and stay in touch with their fans.

Keep in mind that TikTok, unlike other video networks such as Instagram, values authentic content from its creators. Doja Cat, an artist, is one of the personalities on TikTok who has amassed 14.7 million followers by providing content on the platform that demonstrates her unique personality and appears to be authentic. TikTok fans seek authentic content to which they can relate and trust people since they are similar to themselves.

Who are TikTokers?

It is the native TikTokers that are the actual stars; they are names that are less well known in the larger media world but are well known to the majority of 14-year-olds. Many of these famous people came to TikTok from other social media sites like YouTube and Instagram, but they quickly gained a big fan base once they figured out how to use the unique platform style of TikTok.

For instance, FitWaffle, a food influencer who got its start on Instagram, has amassed over 2.5 million followers and over 75 million likes (as of November 2021) on TikTok since the app's inception in 2019. This number is accurate as of November 2021. It was made by Eloise Head, who is one of the most famous and fastest-growing food bloggers in the world.

There is also a large community of creative influencers who use TikTok to reach new audiences around the world, connect with communities that share their interests, and work with brands to promote their products and services while making a good living from the platform. TikTok's selection of beauty, fashion, food, dance, and fitness influencers allows marketers to reach younger audiences without having their own presence on the platform. These influencers understand TikTok's functioning and can develop reactive content that capitalizes on current trends.

The app has helped increase the number of "content houses" or "collab houses," which are places where groups of young social media influencers live together in mansions to make a good setting for their branded viral content. The high rental costs are paid for by talent agents or managers who work with brands to set up deals and contracts. Rihanna's Fenty Beauty company made an investment in a content house in the year 2020. Rihanna hand-picked a team of five content creators to work for the content house. Due to COVID, the event had to be cut short, but the brand's content makers were still promoting it online.

Charli D'Amelio, a 16-year-old TikTok influencer, lived in Hype House, a LA mansion where she was able to gain over 100 million followers. She often works with brands that share her interests and values. For example, she has made products with the beauty brand Morphe and worked with UNICEF to spread anti-bullying messages. She now has the most followers on TikTok, followed by Khaby Lame and Addison Rae. This shows how much TikTok and Instagram influencers have in common.

How Much Do TikTokers Make?

TikTok is the place to be if you are interested in becoming an influencer or using influencer marketing to promote your brand. Because TikTok has grown so quickly, many users have made money on the platform by making creative videos and getting sponsorship deals.

The TikTok Creator's Fund, which was just announced, has expanded the chances available to its users. This fund, which is expected to increase to $2 billion over the following three years, will allow producers with 10,000 followers and 100,000 video views to make money from video views.

TikTok, which has one billion monthly active users, provides content creators with the opportunity to reach a large audience with their creations. It also gives them a place where their content can go viral and be seen by big brands around the world. Who are the most powerful influencers on the platform, how did they achieve such a high level of success, and how much do TikTok users typically earn?

How much do TikTokers make per 1,000 views?

TikTok does not disclose many details about how Creator Fund payouts are calculated. Tubefilter spoke to a number of influencers, including Ryan Shakes and Cheyenne Wise, who reported receiving between two and four cents per 1,000 views from the fund.

That's not a lot of money for Tiktokers with low video views. However, for top TikTokers who frequently create videos and have a large fan base, the Creators Fund might give them an opportunity to make a living and a healthy annual compensation of $100,000 - $200,000.

How Much Do Famous TikTokers make?

There are many TikTok influencers with large followings, but the top 10 TikTokers are in a class by themselves. Top TikTokers like Charli D'Amelio, who is closing in on 130 million followers, have the potential to make millions of dollars per year if the platform's growth continues at its current rate of progress.

TikToker	Followers (as of Oct 2021)	Estimated earnings (per sponsored post) *
Charli D'Amelio	127.6 million	$638,000
Khabane Lame	117.6 million	$588,000
Addision Rae	85.4 million	$423,000
Bella Poarch	84.6 million	$422,500
Zach King	66 million	$330,000
Will Smith	62.4 million	$311,000
Dixie D'Amelio	55.4 million	$277,000
Spencer Polanco Knight	55 million	$275,000
Loren Gray	54.1 million	$270,500
Kimberly Loaiza	53.9 million	$269,000

These influencers have other opportunities to generate revenue beyond only TikTok. Due to their extensive reach, marketers are clamoring to secure endorsement and sponsorship deals with them to advertise their products and services.

Who are The Richest TikTokers?

Let's examine the top Tiktokers in terms of their estimated net worth, annual revenue, and income sources.

Charli D'Amelio

Charli D'Amelio is a household name on TikTok due to the fact that she was the first user to surpass the milestone of 100 million followers. Celebrity Net Worth says that she made $3 million in 2020 and that she charges at least $100,000 per sponsored post. A two-second SuperBowl ad reportedly earned her $1 million.

She is also well-known on Instagram (9.64 million followers) and YouTube (44.6 million followers). The D'Amelio Show, a new reality series depicting her family, debuted on Hulu recently, and she now sells branded items, including hoodies and t-shirts. Not bad for a seventeen-year-old who joined social media only a few years ago.

Dixie D'Amelio

Dixie D'Amelio, Charli's younger sister, made $2.9 million in 2020 from endorsement deals with Hollister and Morphe, as well as relationships with Taco Bell and Crest.

Her sister makes money on TikTok by dancing, but Dixie is a singer. In 2020, she put out her first single, which became the most popular video on YouTube. She is also expected to profit from the reality program alongside her family, in addition to her estimated worth of $4 million.

Addison Rae

Addison Rae's reputation has skyrocketed in recent years as she has mastered TikTok, Instagram, and YouTube. In the year 2020, Forbes projected that she had an impressive income of $5 million. So, how did she do it?

Addison receives between $50,000 and $90,000 for each sponsored post and generates money through her partnership with Hype House, a content producer collective comprised of the world's top influencers.

In addition to that, she has signed contracts with American Eagle, Reebok, and Sephora. All of this, as well as a growing acting career as a result of her TikTok stardom, has resulted in a multi-picture video agreement with Netflix and an exclusive podcast arrangement with Spotify.

Loren Gray

Loren Gray became known through the app Musical.ly, which TikTok bought for its music directory. Her lip-syncing and dancing videos paved the path for a singing career with Virgin and Capitol Records, and Forbes estimates she will earn $2.4 million on TikTok in 2020.

Lauren has sponsorship relationships with Burger King, Hyundai, and Revlon and may earn up to $197,000 for a sponsored article. She also recently established a jewelry collection. Her estimated net worth is $5 million.

Khaby Lame

Italian Khaby Lame created his account in April 2020. He has garnered a large following since then as a result of his inventive and caustic videos. He reportedly charges $50,000 for a promotional video and makes an estimated $200,000 each month.

His popularity has caused marketers to take notice. Aside from Netflix and Barilla, he has also struck arrangements with the fantasy sports platform Dream11, and others are in the works. Khaby just debuted on the runway in his first fashion show, which he co-hosted with Hugo Boss and Russell Athletic.

Bella Poarch

The most popular video of 2020 was about how social influencer Bella Poarch makes money. With approximately 650 million views, her TikTok lip-synching video 'M to the B' drew the attention of users and businesses.

Bella has recently secured a record deal with Warner Records, and she is also a part of a Non-Fungible Tokens (NFT) collection on TikTok, along with other artists. She is similar to many other influencers in that she uploads to various social networks, both organically and sponsored. Her net worth is believed to be $2 million, but it is expected to rise.

Important TikTok Statistics for Marketers in 2022

TikTok, whether you like it or not, is becoming increasingly difficult to ignore. Record-breaking numbers for the app and its audience in 2021 have made it even more popular than ever.

Even though many people still think of it as a place for dance challenges by people in Generation Z, TikTok has grown to include all kinds of content and communities.

The following is a list of the most important TikTok statistics for you to keep in mind as you design your marketing strategy for TikTok in 2022.

With 656 million downloads, TikTok was the most popular app of 2021

This is more than 100 million more downloads than second-place Instagram, which had 545 million downloads last year.

TikTok has also been number one for the past three years in a row. In 2019 there were 693 million downloads, while in 2020, there were 850 million. It saw a significant decline in worldwide downloads from the prior year, similar to many other apps on the most-downloaded list, but managed to maintain its top spot.

Apptopia says that TikTok was also the most downloaded app in the United States in 2021, with 94 million downloads. This is a 6 percent increase over the number of downloads in 2020.

TikTok also kept its spot as the highest-earning app, with more than $2.5 billion spent by users in 2021.

TikTok has received over 3 billion downloads

In July 2021, TikTok had been downloaded three billion times. That's even more astounding when you consider they only achieved two billion downloads a year ago.

It is also the first app that isn't made by Facebook to get 3 billion downloads. Facebook, Messenger, Instagram, and WhatsApp are the only other apps that have done so since January 2014.

Even though TikTok was only released in 2016, it has already become the fifth most popular app of the decade.

TikTok is the 6th most popular social networking site in the world

It trails only Facebook, YouTube, WhatsApp, Instagram, and WeChat when it comes to popularity. It has overcome Facebook Messenger to take the sixth rank in 2021.

Nevertheless, there is another way to view these ranks. Douyin, the Chinese equivalent of TikTok, is ranked eighth on this list. Douyin is the first app created by parent firm ByteDance in September 2016, before TikTok became available to foreign audiences in 2017. There are minor variations between the two applications, but their appearance and functionality are nearly identical.

There are 600 million people using Douyin on a daily basis (most apps use monthly figures). When the two applications are merged, they reach the fourth position on this list, surpassing Instagram and WeChat.

TikTok is controversial among US adults

TikTok has its naysayers: in the United States, 34% of adults have negative opinions of the app, while 37% have positive sentiments. Compared to other platforms, this one is more divisive: Instagram is perceived favorably by 50% of respondents and negatively by 24%. Facebook is seen favorably by 55% of people and negatively by 39%.

Naturally, this varies with age. Among those aged 18 to 34, 59% think favorably of TikTok, compared to 40% among those aged 35 to 44 and 31% among those aged 45 to 64. Older populations are more skeptical than younger ones.

This apprehension may be due to the platform's history of displaying upsetting information. In December of 2021, a school violence fake circulated swiftly on TikTok, frightening parents and students. Other frauds and hazardous content, such as videos advertising rapid weight loss, have flourished and received criticism on the network.

Because of this, in February 2022, TikTok announced safety improvements to its Community Guidelines. They have made a commitment to eliminating harmful information on the site, paying special attention to anything that encourages violent or suicidal behavior, eating disorders, or self-harm.

TikTok has nearly one billion active monthly users

To say TikTok is rapidly increasing is an understatement. Every second, eight new people join TikTok, and every day, an average of 650,000 new people join. No big deal, just everyone in Helsinki signing up every day.

Those figures pile up quickly. TikTok's main company, ByteDance, said in September 2021 that they had reached one billion users, a 45 percent growth over July 2020. TikTok reached a billion users in under five years, but Facebook and YouTube each required eight years to reach the milestone. More than that, by the end of 2022, TikTok is predicted to have 1.5 billion users.

TikTok users engage with other social media networks

Users of social media are active across a variety of platforms: users between the ages of 18 and 34 utilize an average of 8 sites on a monthly basis. Similar to other sites, 99.9 percent of TikTok users report using other platforms.

TikTok users are most prevalent on Facebook (84.6 percent overlap), Instagram (83.9 percent overlap), and YouTube (80.5 percent overlap).

TikTok has surpassed Instagram in popularity among US Gen Z users

With 37.3 million users compared to Instagram's 33.3 million, TikTok has now eclipsed Instagram in terms of popularity among users who are members of Gen Z (those born between 1997 and 2012) in the United States.

However, TikTok is also making significant progress in other age groupings. For example, in the first three months of 2021, 36 percent of TikTok users were between the ages of 35 and 54, which is an increase from 26 percent in the same time period in 2020.

Gen Z still uses Snapchat more than Instagram and TikTok, but by 2025, all three apps should have about the same number of users.

The majority of TikTok's users are female

A whopping 57% of TikTok's global user population is female. This percentage jumps to 61 percent among TikTok users in the United States.

While TikTok's user base is becoming more varied, companies aiming to attract younger female viewers will likely find the best results.

TikTok isn't anyone's favorite app

Surprisingly, only 4.3 percent of internet users identified TikTok as their preferred social media platform. This is fewer than a third of those who preferred Instagram (14.8 percent) or Facebook (14.5 percent)

And despite the fact that TikTok is widely known for its leadership position in the market for members of Generation Z, it is not the most popular option among younger users. Instagram is the app of choice for the vast majority of users who are between the ages of 16 and 24. This includes 22.8 percent of male users and 25.6 percent of female users. Only 8.9% of female users in this age group chose TikTok as their favorite app, and only 5.4% of male users did the same.

TikTok is used for 19.6 hours a month by Android users

When compared to the amount of time Android users spent on the app in 2020, which was 13.3 hours per month, this is a 47% increase in the amount of time spent on the app.

TikTok and Facebook are neck-and-neck in usage time. YouTube maintains its position as the most popular video-sharing website, as users stay engaged with the platform for an average of 23.7 hours per month.

The usage differs from country to country. With an average usage time of 27.3 hours, UK users are the most active on TikTok. Users in the United States spend somewhat more time on TikTok than their Canadian counterparts (22.6 hours per month on average).

TikTok is by far the most engaging social networking app

It's impossible not to be engaged by TikTok if you've ever opened the app for a single video and then closed it again an hour later. In fact, users spend an average of 10.85 minutes on TikTok, making it the most interesting social media app.

When compared to Pinterest, the app with the second-most engaging user experience, which averages 5.06 minutes per session, is more than twice as long. At an average of 2.95 minutes per session, it is also significantly longer than the amount of time that users generally spend on Instagram.

TikTok is mostly used by the majority of users to locate humorous or amusing content, according to a 2022 GlobalWebIndex survey question.

The second most frequent habit is posting or sharing content, while the third most frequent activity is following the news. Instagram and Snapchat, on the other hand, were mostly used to post content. So, it may be safe to say that TikTok's main selling point, especially when it comes to using, is its entertainment value.

Instagram, Pinterest, Reddit, Twitter, and Snapchat are other social networks where users can access humorous or interesting content. But only TikTok and Reddit ranked highest for this usage scenario.

430 TikTok tunes topped 1 billion views in 2021

On TikTok, music is more popular than ever before. There were three times as many songs with over one billion views in 2019 as there were in 2020. Seventy-five percent of TikTok users claim they find new songs on the app, and 73 percent of users identify certain songs with TikTok, according to a new survey. Many of these songs also achieved mainstream success; in 2021, 175 tracks were both TikTok trends and Billboard Hot 100 chart-toppers.

According to the TikTok's, What's Next Report 2022, 88 percent of users indicate that music is an integral part of the TikTok experience. Perhaps this is why audio is used in 93 percent of the top-performing videos.

Users are now viewing lengthier videos

Up until recently, TikTok videos could only be 60 seconds long. In July 2021, however, TikTok began allowing users to upload videos up to three minutes in length, followed by 10 minutes in 2022.

In October, TikTok said that videos longer than one minute had already been watched more than five billion times around the world. Longer videos are more popular with users in Vietnam, Thailand, and Japan, while shorter videos are most popular with users in the United States, United Kingdom, and Brazil.

TikTok is also expanding its video viewing options with the launch of TikTok TV in November 2021. It is expected that TikTok will experience a comparable rise in reach and engagement, given that more than half of YouTube users watch content on a TV screen.

Finance TikTok increased by 255 percent in 2021

Investing, cryptocurrencies and all things financial had a big year, according to TikTok's What's Next Report 2022. Views of videos with the hashtag #NFT increased by a mind-boggling 93,000 percent in comparison to 2020. With 1.9 billion views, the hashtag #crypto also went viral. Financial themes are prone to TikTok's crazy inclinations, as shown by the #TikTokDogeCoinChallenge.

On the app, there is also a vibrant and expanding personal finance community.

The success of FinTok shows that any industry can establish a presence in the app if they produce high-quality content, regardless of whether your brand has anything to do with finance. No matter what your brand's niche is, you can be sure that your customers are on the app.

TikTok is typically dismissed as childish entertainment, yet young people utilize it to educate themselves. Short, approachable video content offers a gateway into subjects like inflation that could otherwise be scary (which also saw a 1900 percent increase in views last year).

TikTok is the most popular app for customer spending

TikTok has surpassed Tinder to become the number one app for generating customer spending, according to AppAnnie.

In 2021, people's spending on TikTok went up by a huge 77 percent. Overall, people spent $2.3 billion on the app, which is more than the $1.3 billion they spent on the app the year before.

TikTok advertising is seen by 884.9 million people, or 15.9% of the global population over 18, which represents 17.9% of all internet users who are 18 or older.

TikTok has the greatest reach among Gen Z users, with 25% of females and 17% of males between the ages of 18 and 24 using the app.

Reach varies from country to country. In the United States, a TikTok ad could reach 50.3% of adults or 130,962,500 people. The US, Indonesia, Brazil, Russia, and Mexico are among the countries where advertising could reach the most people.

Marketers are becoming more convinced that TikTok works

TikTok is making significant advances as marketers evaluate where to put their limited ad expenditures. According to Hootsuite's 2022 Social Trends Survey, 24 percent of marketers said TikTok was beneficial for accomplishing their business goals, up from 3 percent the previous year - a 700 percent increase.

It is still far behind the advertising behemoths Facebook and Instagram. However, between 2020 and 2021, both platforms witnessed a considerable reduction in perceived effectiveness: Facebook by 25% and Instagram by 40%.

These shifts signal an evolving ad landscape, and firms must adapt to meet customers on each channel. TikTok provides a wide range of niche communities, from bookworms to fridge tinkerers, that allow marketers to target certain demographics.

Creator partnerships increase click-through rates by 193%

Creators, the TikTok marketplace's official influencers, are one of the platform's most valuable assets for businesses. Through the TikTok Creator Marketplace, brands can collaborate with over 100,000 creators to create content that targets their target audiences. This is good for both users and brands: 35% of users find new products and brands through creators, and 65% of users like it when creators talk about products and brands.

Benefit Cosmetics collaborated with the founders of the Benefit Brow Challenge in one case study to market their new Brow Micro filling Pen. The 22 videos produced by Gen Z and Millennial videomakers received 1.4 million impressions and over 3500 hours of viewing time.

The "infinite loop" of TikTok is revolutionizing online shopping

TikTok content has historically had a strong influence on viewers' shopping behavior. You only have to look at the TikTok Feta Effect to see proof. But until recently, this effect was indirect: users would find out about a product through the app but then buy it somewhere else.

That was the case until August 2021, when TikTok and Shopify announced a new integration that would enable shopping within the app.

But the shift is broader than just click-to-buy. TikTok considers the retail process to be an eternal loop rather than a marketing funnel. For example, the journey does not end with a purchase—it continues on, with customers sharing their experiences and promoting the product to friends and family. After making a purchase, one user out of every four has written a post about their newly acquired item, and one user out of every five has created a video tutorial.

67% of users claim TikTok makes them shop when they weren't going to

Users of TikTok enjoy communicating with brands; in fact, 73 percent of users have reported that they have a closer connection to businesses that they contact on the platform.

TikTok's own user behavior data indicates the extent of its impact on customers' purchasing patterns. 37% of people who find a product via the app immediately want to purchase it. And 29 percent of users have attempted to purchase an item from the app only to discover that it was sold out – that's the TikTok Feta Effect in action. So, it's not surprising that the hashtag #TikTokMadeMeBuyIt got over 7.4 billion views in 2021.

The best-performing videos have a duration of 21 to 34 secs

In this sweet zone, video impressions increase by 1.6%, which is tiny but substantial.

The addition of captions boosts the number of views by 55.7 percent

Text in your video is more than simply a good idea for inclusive design. It also has considerable advantages over videos that do not have captions or a call-to-action.

Another increasing TikTok trend? Voice effects. In videos with text-to-speech capability enabled, TikTok generates an auto-generated voiceover of the visible text. As of December 2021, videos with the hashtag #VoiceEffects had received 160 billion views.

While voice-to-text is an amazing technology that expands video accessibility and reach, many people dislike the voice. The message is that marketers should invest in high-quality captioning and narration to guarantee their videos reach and appeal to the widest possible audience.

WHAT IS TIKTOK MARKETING?

Marketing on TikTok refers to the process of advertising different goods and services to end-users of the platform. Common ways to market on TikTok are to create organic content based on trends, use popular hashtags, and include TikTok influencers in marketing campaigns.

Marketing on TikTok can help businesses:

- Increase brand recognition
- Create active communities
- Offer products and services for sale
- Obtain customer and audience feedback
- Improve customer service
- Promote your goods and services to the right people

Why Should You Use Tiktok to Market Products?

The main difference between TikTok and other social media platforms, like Facebook and Instagram, is that the homepages of the latter two are mostly made up of people you already know and channels you already follow. TikTok, on the other hand, prioritizes videos from new and unknown creators.

TikTok's user experience keeps customers in the app longer than Facebook and Twitter. You can also include a "Link in bio" on TikTok, making it easy to market and monetize.

TikTok is a very excellent tool for reaching a younger demographic—62 percent of its viewership is between the ages of 10 and 29. With this information, you can tailor your videos to the content Gen Z enjoys and use your knowledge of the algorithm to generate virality.

Here are a few of the advantages of using TikTok for marketing.

Every video has the potential to go viral

A lot of people have criticized Facebook's algorithm over the last few years since it's so different from other social networks. Since then, the company has pledged to prioritize feeds for friends and family. This means that it gives the most weight to people and things you already know.

TikTok works in the opposite direction, prioritizing videos from creators you've never seen before. This discovery engine ensures that every video, regardless of how many followers its creator may already have, has the potential to become an internet sensation and spread like wildfire.

TikTok brings content to more people in a new and different way. TikTok has confirmed that the number of a user's followers does not directly influence the content that is displayed in their feed. This is in contrast to the majority of social media platforms, which make the decision regarding what content to serve you largely based on the popularity of the poster.

What exactly does this mean? In essence, you may become an overnight success by uploading just one video. Without considering follower counts, the newcomer has the same probability of going viral as the mega-pop star.

So, what is the secret behind TikTok's virality? A lot of it boils down to simply jumping on something that is already popular.

You'll notice that a lot of the videos on the platform use the same tunes and hashtags after only a short while. When you notice that, ask yourself if your brand can join the trend. You can also initiate new trends by creating your own hashtags.

People buy what they see

Whether you utilize TikTok advertisements, brand takeovers, or regularly post videos about your product, there is a significant probability that someone will notice and purchase it. According to research conducted by Adweek, almost half of the people who use the TikTok app end up making purchases from the companies they see within the application.

The term and hashtag "TikTok made me buy that" came into being as a direct result of product-based social media trends that originated with TikTok. Forty-nine percent of those polled said it's becoming a more important marketing tool for retailers throughout the holiday season.

Influencer marketing on TikTok is huge

According to Statista, the market for influencer marketing on a global scale has more than doubled since 2019 and is projected to reach $13.8 billion in 2021. More brands see the value of collaborating with creators to market their products and services.

TikTok's content producers have the potential to garner millions of fans. What's more, the best part? On the platform, niches operate nicely. Because of this, when a subculture begins to gain traction on the app, it is given its very own TikTok space and given names like Goth TikTok, Gay TikTok, and NYC TikTok, for example.

As with any form of influencer marketing, the key to success is selecting the perfect person to represent your business. But with these well-known niches, it's easy to find people who have a lot of influence in your space.

CEOs are also becoming artists in order to boost their brand marketing initiatives. The founder of August, Nadya Okamoto, has built her personal account in parallel with the growth of the brand account. She claims that making herself the influencer has been a more effective marketing strategy for August. The majority of the time, Nadya uses her account to test out new content and respond to frequently asked queries pertaining to her products.

The distinction between a brand and its creator is now critically vital for awareness. Business accounts don't have access to as many of the trending audios that they can use, which can increase the virality of a brand.

Furthermore, if your items primarily appeal to a younger audience (13 to 24), TikTok is an ideal choice. A massive 69 percent of all TikTok users are aged 13 to 24, with 27 percent aged 13 to 17 and 42 percent aged 18 to 24. TikTok is a golden ticket if you want to reach this group.

Finding users on TikTok that are a good fit for your brand is going to be the most challenging aspect of getting started with influencer marketing on that platform. It's important to check the specialization of the influencer before using TikTok marketing; for example, a male fitness influencer would be a poor choice for a female fitness program.

TikTok is compatible with Instagram

Here's the good news if you've already established a presence on Instagram: TikTok offers built-in tools that connect to Instagram. To begin, there is a connection button for Instagram located on your profile (which is separate from the external link option). This makes it easy for people to go to your Instagram from your TikTok.

Second, there is automated Instagram sharing. TikTok now has the option to automatically broadcast your videos to Instagram Stories and/or your Instagram Feed, if you choose.

Content Variety

TikTok is a new medium for expressing oneself online and is more than just a social network in its own right. As vinyl records propelled the two-minute single to mainstream success, TikTok will do the same for bite-sized media. As a result, content makers will need to become familiar with TikTok's features.

This means that Facebook and Instagram postings cannot be imported directly into TikTok and vice versa. In spite of the fact that you will need to increase the amount of time you put into social media, this opens the door for you to try out new concepts that you normally wouldn't test on other platforms.

TikTok is all about music and video, whereas Twitter and Instagram are focused on text and photos, respectively. It's difficult to make a great TikTok post without engaging audio and eye-catching images.

The most popular posts on TikTok are typically related to one of two categories: comedy or music. While there are some serious uploads, most users use TikTok to watch short, loopable comedic snippets or videos (especially dance routines) matched to popular melodies.

As a consequence of this, TikTok is an extremely casual platform; hence, coming off as overly professional or salesy will not go over well with your audience. Although you may keep a business-like demeanor on Instagram, you'll undoubtedly want to loosen up and have fun with yourself if you're posting to TikTok.

Despite the fact that consistent branding is typical of the utmost significance, it fails in this circumstance. To summarize, don't be scared to be innovative and step outside of your comfort zone. Create content that encourages users to interact with one another, such as amusing videos, quick dance routines, branded and unbranded hashtag challenges (free and organic), and so on.

If you truly want your work to be remembered, keep up with the current TikTok trends. This will provide you with a decent indication of which songs and effects are popular, allowing you to ride the wave with your .

TikTok Is Not Oversaturated

TikTok is a platform that is still very new. It was released in 2016 but didn't become popular until its parent business merged it with Musical.ly in 2018. This opens the door for fresh ideas and voices on TikTok. Despite having a sizable following on Instagram and Facebook, a great number of well-known firms have not yet moved their operations to TikTok. When it comes to marketing and business, TikTok is still in the early adopter stage. This is true from both a customer and a business standpoint. For newcomers to the platform, there is a lower level of rivalry and fewer famous names competing for the same audience.

Just because a market isn't overly crowded doesn't mean success is guaranteed. There's a good chance that many well-known people don't have profiles on TikTok because they don't know what kind of content to make.

That is totally fair given that TikTok for Business is still in its infancy, and in order for it to be successful, users will need to be forward-thinking and aware of current cultural trends. The wrong kind of content will make you look like a joke.

Is there a way out? Get on the platform, begin watching content, and start being creative. Since there are currently no guidelines, you should experiment with new things and see where they take you.

Types of Brands Used for Marketing on TikTok

The three main methods of marketing that businesses use on TikTok are listed below.

TikTok influencer marketing

A large element of TikTok's ecology is its influencer marketing efforts. Mega-stars like Charli D'Amelio, Addison Rae, and Zach King have a significant influence on a business's ability to succeed. However, a high-profile influencer is not required for successful marketing; instead, look for budding stars or influencers in your industry. For example, a small cosmetics firm based in Vancouver might use the hashtag #vancouvermakeup to discover influencers such as Sarah McNabb.

Making your own TikTok videos

This choice provides the most flexibility. Make a Business TikTok account for your business (scroll down for thorough step-by-step instructions) and begin creating your own organic content.

The sky is definitely the limit here; you may upload anything from product demos to day-in-the-life videos to dancing challenges. Spend some time looking at your "For You" page to get ideas.

TikTok advertising

If you're searching for a starting point and have some money to invest, this is it: TikTok's website is filled with success stories from firms who began advertising on TikTok, such as Aerie, Little Caesars, and Maybelline. TikTok advertising, like those on Facebook and Instagram, is priced using a bidding approach.

TikTok for Business

TikTok launched a TikTok for Business hub in the summer of 2020, followed by TikTok Pro a few months later.

Initially, there was a separation between the two—one for businesses, the other for growth-savvy creators—but because both hubs produced nearly identical insights, TikTok eventually blended them.

At this point, the only option available is TikTok for Business. Access to real-time stats and audience insights is possible only with a business account.

TikTok for Business: Getting Started

TikTok for Business accounts can be created in four simple steps. Even better: It's completely free.

1. Create a TikTok account: Get the app from the Apple App Store or the Google Play Store and sign up for an account.
2. Create a TikTok business account
3. Improve your TikTok profile: Select a distinct username and display name, as well as a profile image that best symbolizes your brand. Finally, include a brief description of your brand and include your website's URL in the bio box to encourage visitors from the social media platform to visit you.
4. Start sharing your content.
   You also have the option of connecting your Instagram account to your

TikTok profile, which will assist you in converting your fans across several platforms.

How to create a TikTok business name

- Navigate to your profile.
- Click the cogwheel in the upper right corner to access the Settings and Privacy option.
- Select Manage Account.
- Select Switch to Business Account from the Account Control menu.
- Tiktok has a wide variety of categories, ranging from "Art & Crafts" to "Personal Blog" to "Fitness" to "Machinery & Equipment," so you can select the one that most accurately represents your account.
- From there, you can add a website and email address for your business to your profile, and you're good to go.

The Business Creative Hub and TikTok Shopping are two of the unique in-app services that are available to users with business accounts. These features are aimed to assist small businesses.

The Business Creative Hub (link) was established to help business users be inspired when developing TikTok content. It provides content development guides and regularly shares popular information to assist everyone, from seasoned professionals to novices. The Creative Hub is a terrific resource for learning about the most effective ways to get users to engage with your app. In order to access the Business Creative Hub, go to the "Business suite" section of the "Settings and Privacy" menu that is included within the app.

TikTok Shopping is an integrated e-commerce platform that does not require users to exit the application in order to make product purchases. When a person has enabled TikTok Shopping, their profile will display a dedicated shopping tab denoted by a little bag.

Developing a Marketing Strategy for TikTok Businesses

Follow these instructions to develop your TikTok marketing plan to make sure your efforts are directed and will help you achieve your marketing and commercial objectives.

Define your target audience

Although Gen Z users represent a significant portion of TikTok's user base, Gen Z as a whole is simply too diverse to be considered a "defined audience."

You don't have to list every characteristic, but try to provide enough information to create a picture of the people who are most likely to become clients. This is your intended audience.

Location: Where do your ideal customers actually live? Knowing only the country can be beneficial. However, if your firm is local or you just want to serve a particular region, you should focus on that area.

Age: What is your customer's age range? Unless you are positive that your target customer is at a specific moment in their life, keep this as wide as possible.

Gender: How do people identify? Depending on your brand, this may be irrelevant or critical.

Interests: What are their hobbies and passions? These are useful for generating prospective content ideas and for targeting audiences (e.g., cooking, hip-hop dance, yoga).

What profession/industry do they work in? What positions have they held? Again, depending on your brand, this may not be as important.

Income range: What is this buyer persona's income range? Do they care about price, or are they willing to pay more for better products?

Relationship status: Are they single, in a relationship, or married? If you work in the wedding business, for example, this could be important to you.

Favorite websites/apps: What kinds of websites do they bookmark? Do they use Instagram or Pinterest on a regular basis? Are there any apps they can't live without?

Purchase motivation: What reasons would this person have for purchasing your product? What would motivate this person to buy your product? What are some of the reasons that come to mind? Do they want to flaunt a status symbol or make time to exercise despite a hectic schedule?

Customer concerns: What are the reasons why they would not purchase your product? Are they concerned about the standard?

Other information: Anything not mentioned but worth mentioning, such as education, life stage (parents with newborn children), activities attended, etc.

Recognize the environment

On TikTok, you face competition from two different types of users: your business competition (whom you have probably already recognized) and your content competition. Because TikTok, like other social media platforms, is populated with users and brands alike, you will not only be competing with other businesses but also with other users who create content.

Look at the businesses that are competing with you and see if they are on TikTok. If they do, examine the different kinds of content they post and determine which of their posts receive a considerable amount of engagement. This can provide you with valuable insight into the preferences of their audience, which is likely to be relatively comparable to the preferences of your audience. Just keep in mind that the stuff you create should be original; copying others' ideas is not allowed here.

Spend some time perusing the content that is already available on TikTok to get an idea of what is being made in your area. Look for topics related to your brand by searching hashtags, joining groups, and viewing trending postings. Take note of any overlaps between these posts and your business competition.

Develop a strategy for promotion

In addition to putting time and effort into making your TikTok profile and videos look like your brand, you can boost your TikTok marketing with paid advertising and influencers.

Influencer marketing exposes your brand and products to the audience of a third party, functioning as social proof. And given TikTok is a creator-focused network like Snapchat, influencer marketing is huge.

Peace Out Skincare used an influencer to advertise its acne line. The company gave some of its wares to TikTok influencers, and two of those influencers worked together on a video.

Over 12 million people saw, and 2.4 million people liked the video in just one day, and $15,000 worth of products were sold. The video remained popular for months after its first upload, resulting in a constant stream of sales beyond the initial boom.

Scout influencers on the platform to determine who resonates with your business and audience before incorporating them into your TikTok marketing campaign. Reach out to users directly using the platform's messaging system and offer to give them free products in exchange for a video of the user's experience and candid feedback. This is fantastic for marketing and product teams.

In terms of paid advertising, TikTok Adverts Manager gives you access to a range of tools that can assist you in increasing the visibility of your ads to a specific audience. Omolola Jewellery, a business that sells on Shopify, reaches out to new users by publishing both organic and paid posts on TikTok. During the pandemic, when clients were unable to visit Omolola's physical store, this proved to be particularly useful in maintaining and growing the company's business.

Become a Pro user to access more data

It's simple to become engrossed in the thrilling process of developing and putting content ideas into action in digital marketing. However, TikTok marketing is more than just creating viral content. Creating a brand is one thing; creating a brand that brings in money is another.

It all starts with understanding what metrics to track and why. Fortunately, content creators may make use of the precise information that Pro TikTok accounts (which can be created for free) provide regarding their followers, traffic, and interaction. You can see information for things like:

- Seven-day and 28-day looks back at the number of followers
- Video metrics such as views, playtime, likes, and comments are tracked.
- Profile View
- Traffic Source
- Gender, region, age, and other demographics of the audience
- Other content that your target audience enjoys (videos and sounds)
- Your most popular videos

You can also check out global data points, such as views of hashtags, and use the Discover tab to see what topics are currently popular.

So, how does all of this affect your bottom line? TikTok marketing is mostly focused on increasing brand awareness. It is a platform that can be used to bring your company in front of a younger audience, and you should continue to develop content in order to keep them involved and to maintain yourself at the forefront of their minds.

You can use TikTok to cultivate relationships with young people who are potential customers, with the expectation that these ties will, in the future, bear fruit in the shape of actual customer-brand relationships.

TikTok users do not want to be sold to; they want to be amused or enlightened.

You should also make sure to let your fans know where else on the web you are active so that they can keep up with your adventure and participate in it. Having your TikTok fans investigate your other channels is an excellent way to expand your personal or corporate brand. Don't forget to share your TikTok link on other social media platforms.

TikTok Marketing Tips

Now that you've determined your approach, it's time to put it into action. You can use these suggestions when developing and sharing content on TikTok, so keep them in mind.

Be real

Be yourself and stand out from the crowd with your content on TikTok, where there's a lot of competition. Your videos shouldn't sound like sales pitches, as this is not what TikTok is for. TikTok users like to be amused or informed rather than marketed to.

Spend some time on TikTok before beginning your TikTok marketing activities. Once the algorithm knows what you like, it will show you good content that you might find inspiring. This can help you come up with new ideas for your own videos.

This app was built to feel like an online community of people sharing relevant and honest content. Users may be turned off by 4K videos, elaborate edits, and "cinematic" or "corporate" TikTok videos.

It's acceptable for your page to feel less brand-consistent than the rest of your social media channels because most content is shot, edited, and uploaded using a smartphone. Some companies, such as Chipotle and Wendy's, are quite good at exchanging their otherwise well-crafted corporate messaging for an authentic connection with a significant number of their customers and fans.

Get your gear

After trying my hand at a number of different approaches to the process of making video , I've determined that the best way to record videos is to use the TikTok app on an iPhone. It's possible to compensate for poor lighting or a distracting background by using the app's beauty filters and lighting choices.

Some of the videos that I've made were assembled in Adobe Premiere, and then they were exported into TikTok. The amount of time necessary to develop this content was not worth the outcomes, despite the fact that a few of these videos have been successful. This may or may not be true for your cluster.

However, sound is not something that should be compromised. Even though your iPhone's built-in mic might work fine, good audio goes a long way toward getting more views and shares.

Go live

Using TikTok's LIVE function, which allows artists to communicate directly with followers via a live stream, is one method to make a personal connection with your audience. One of the most effective methods to distinguish yourself on TikTok is to go live.

When you begin a live stream, the app will notify your followers by sending a notification on their For You pages and pinning your stream to the top. Because there are currently millions of creators using the site, this real estate is extremely valuable. TikTok strongly emphasizes the going-live option, which is surprisingly simple to implement.

When it comes to live streaming, it's very normal to feel overwhelmed or maybe a little shy. "What if I make a mistake?" "What if I don't know how to respond to a question?" These are common anxieties that we all have, but they often vanish as soon as you press the Go Live button.

To soothe your worries, make a list of talking points for common queries and update it after each TikTok LIVE. During a LIVE, do your best to answer any acceptable questions, and be sure to thank fans who "give" you stickers/emojis, as these have a tiny monetary value. Consider it slightly more aesthetically pleasing than users giving you a nickel for making interesting content.

Scheduling is also extremely crucial. While impromptu live streams are fun, creating a following for your broadcast is easier if you keep to a regular schedule. Q&A sessions, behind-the-scenes videos, informal hangout streaming, "work with me" sessions, lessons, and interviews with special guests are all fantastic formats. Some creators' weekly live sessions let them connect with their viewers while also pleasing the TikTok algorithm.

When planning a live stream schedule, consider your followers' time zones and choose a time when most people aren't at school or work. When you're initially starting out, this is a terrific strategy to increase viewership.

Keep it simple

You can't write a whole book in a tweet, and you can't make a whole movie in a TikTok. Your videos should be brief and sweet in order to keep your content digestible.

Stick to 15-second videos for high-level information and 60-second deep dives for more in-depth explanations. In the event that a subject is of the utmost significance, you are free to divide it up into several videos that are only 15 seconds long in order to maintain a high level of audience and the opportunity to replay the videos.

Imagine that every piece of content you publish is a different tale that you're telling to your audience. If there isn't enough content, they might not be happy, but if it is too much, you might lose interest.

Since most of the videos on my For You page are between seven and ten seconds long, a 60-second upload will feel like a movie, which many users can't pay attention to.

Making use of calls to action rather than ending your video with an introduction is an excellent method to remind viewers who you are and encourage them to click on your profile for more information.

Videos that are longer than 30 seconds will have a small white bar at the bottom of the screen that shows how much of the video is still playing. If your video is just a few seconds short of 30 seconds, you might want to add a few seconds to get that feature. This will let users know when your video will end, which can keep their attention for longer.

Join the conversation in the comments

TikTok's discovery algorithm does a great job of showing your video to people who might want to follow you, but that's only half the battle. Once the algorithm has piqued someone's attention, it's your duty to keep them hooked.

The comments section on TikTok is an excellent spot for carrying on a conversation, communicating with others, and providing explanations. Participate in the comments section as much as you can to interact with your audience.

Your comments will be accompanied by a Creator badge next to your username, making audience participation extremely visible to potential followers (you'd be astonished at how many people are ecstatic to see a Liked by Creator message appear on their screen). You can also give a comment a thumbs up if you wish to recognize it but don't feel the need to provide a response in writing.

As your postings gain traction and responding to comments becomes too time-consuming, address them at scale. Create a document that categorizes common comments and the sorts to which you might fairly respond. Then, in a lengthier video, a live stream, or a video answer, respond to repeated comments.

TikTok also has extensive filtering capabilities to make your life easier by automatically eliminating comments that contain specific keywords or phrases.

TikTok keeps track of how many comments and views each of your videos get. Based on how smart its algorithm is, it's likely that it also keeps track of how many comments are ignored and how many people respond to them.

Users will find it difficult to overlook a simple like or remark answer if you have a verified account. A new follower is often gained by liking a comment. If you repeat this process a couple of hundred times, you will have successfully converted a constant stream of potential customers into followers.

There is no justification for not responding to each and every remark until your channel has expanded to the point where it is no longer feasible, given how vital comments are to the TikTok experience. This is something that few brands do, so you'll stand out.

It is not only acceptable but even encouraged to delete comments that are inappropriate. You can accomplish this by holding the plus sign (+) and then selecting the delete option.

Understand the trends

Before you submit any content, you should first browse the Discover page on TikTok and determine whether or not you can create content that is congruent with the TikTok trends or hashtag challenges of the day. This will satisfy TikTok's algorithm and increase your following count.

While we don't recommend utilizing these hashtags if your video is completely off subject, it may be a wonderful way to see what's popular on the platform and how to better build your content strategy.

Trending hashtags vary on a regular basis and are an excellent illustration of what keeps TikTok content interesting and entertaining. While writing draft posts is fine, keeping an eye on what's trending is a wonderful approach to demonstrate relevance and appear more personable to your followers.

If you see a certain sound appearing on your For You page several times, get creative and see if you can utilize it in one of your own videos. You can always save it to your favorite sounds for later usage as you brainstorm.

TikTok is not like other social networks in that it does not rely on people searching hashtags and keywords to locate content to consume. Instead, it uses a feature called "clusters" to deliver videos that users will enjoy directly to the For You page.

In this case, a cluster is a group of people who like the same kinds of videos that you do. Maybe they've commented on similar videos, like the same music, or used the app similarly.

You can use hashtags to distribute your videos to certain groups but not to gain views. Some hashtags have inflated counts of views, which might distort the true popularity of a hashtag.

TikTok once displayed the Entrepreneur hashtag on its Explore page. As a result, millions of users created videos with the hashtag "#entrepreneur" in the bio, expecting to gain a few additional video views, even if their content had nothing to do with entrepreneurship.

This method dilutes the hashtag's relevant videos, lowering the hashtag's popularity. To get more views, use popular hashtags in your video content creation, but only if the topic is related to your video and your cluster itself.

Legibility and accessibility

There's a reason why successful TikTok users include titles at the beginning of their videos. When you look at their profile, it's easy to get a sneak peek of what's to come. You can increase the number of people watching your videos by using different colored titles to organize the content of your videos into categories that viewers can more easily navigate to find stuff that may be of interest to them.

It is important to keep in mind that the user interface for TikTok is superimposed on the bottom and right sides of your screen; as a result, you should ensure that the titles you use fall in the center of the screen. Because different types of phones utilize varying aspect ratios, it is helpful to keep key away from the screen's corners in order to maximize the likelihood that it will be viewed by everybody.

Use closed captions wherever feasible to ensure that your videos are accessible to all TikTok users. This ensures that your videos are available to all audiences and settings. This is made quite simple by the app's timed text feature, and it just takes a few more minutes.

Features, features, and more features

TikTok is always adding new features. Some of the most popular ones are animated GIF stickers, new titles, and new filters. Therefore, because the algorithm is a well-guarded secret, you should concentrate on making use of these new capabilities in order to maintain the appearance of originality for your audience.

In addition, we recommend that you check out TikTok's beta program, as it may provide you with additional content-creation capabilities that most users haven't yet discovered. This can help you remain on top of the platform's latest developments and stay ahead of the competition.

Consistent posting

Again, we don't know how the algorithm works, but many content creators have reported incredible success after committing to a regular posting schedule. We recommend updating once or twice a day and going live once or twice a week at the very least. This rhythm keeps your content fresh and entertaining without overloading your audience with videos.

Analyze your analytics to see when your audience is most engaged based on who you're speaking to and where they are situated.

Influencer Marketing Hub examined more than one hundred thousand TikTok posts for engagement trends and determined the optimal posting times, all in Eastern time:

- Monday at 6:00 am, 10:00 am, and 10:00 pm.
- Tuesday at 2:00 am, 4:00 am, and 9:00 am.
- Wednesday at 7:00 am, 8:00 AM, and 11:00 pm.

- Thursday at 9:00 am, 12:00 am, and 7:00 pm.
- Friday at 5:00 am, 1:00 pm, and 3:00 pm.
- Saturday at 11 am, 7 p.m., and 8 pm.
- Sunday at 7:00 am, 8:00 am, and 4:00 pm.

But wait, don't schedule those TikTok posts just yet! Your expanding audience in places like Australia and California, for example, will have varied time zones to take into account. As a global platform, the times and days will vary depending on the country from which people are viewing it. Plus, TikTok doesn't have a way to schedule posts or connect to management apps that do.

Using a time zone converter is the best approach to account for different nations that are important to your brand's customers. Then you can create a content plan for each territory. It's not always easy, but localizing content is a terrific method to encourage TikTok growth.

If your followers are more active on particular days of the week, you may want to consider posting twice on certain days to increase exposure. Since so many new videos are continually being uploaded to the platform, it is essential to continue feeding the algorithm fresh, engaging content.

While determining a "required weekly output" of TikTok is practically difficult, I do know that the algorithm likes consistency. Make sure that whatever rhythm you and your team settle on can be sustained for the foreseeable future, regardless of whatever approach you take.

Join creator communities

There are innumerable TikTok-focused Facebook groups, and many of them are filled with creatives who want to improve their skills. Consider what best suits you and join a community of makers. Being in the company of like-minded individuals is a terrific way to gain inspiration, develop accountability, and stay motivated in the following weeks and months.

If you operate a business, you should look for a TikTok group that focuses on marketing or business strategy. Find comparable communities online if you're a comedian.

If you are unable to discover something that caters to your specific demographic, this may be the ideal chance for you to establish your very own community.

UNDERSTANDING THE TIKTOK ALGORITHM

The algorithm behind TikTok is essentially a recommendation engine that selects the videos that will show up on your For You page.

On your For You page, no two people will see exactly the same videos, and the videos you watch may change over time based on your viewing choices and even your present mood.

TikTok's own definition of the algorithm behind the TikTok For You page is as follows:

"A stream of videos customized to your interests, making it simple to find content and creators you love... driven by a recommendation algorithm that offers content to each user that is likely to be of interest to that specific user."

What is The TikTok Algorithm?

Initially, social media sites kept their algorithms hidden. This makes sense, given that the recommendation engine is a patented technology that contributes to the uniqueness of each social network.

Algorithms are an important technique for social networks to lure us in and keep us interested. TikTok does not want spammers and other nefarious characters to be able to manipulate the algorithm in order to gain more attention than they deserve.

However, in response to people's growing skepticism regarding the inner workings of social networks, the majority of platforms have made the fundamentals of their algorithms publicly available.

Fortunately, this implies that we now have direct knowledge of some of the most important ranking signals used by the TikTok algorithm. They are as follows:

User interactions

TikTok's algorithm is quite similar to the Instagram algorithm in that it bases suggestions on a user's activity within the app and how they interact with different types of content. Which kind of interactions? Anything that reveals the user's preferred content.

The "For You" page suggests content based on a number of things, such as:

- Accounts that you follow
- Creators you've hidden
- Comments you've posted
- Videos on the app that you have liked or shared
- Videos you have marked as favorites
- Videos that have been marked "Not interested."
- Inappropriate videos that you've flagged.
- Longer videos that you watch all the way through (aka video completion rate)
- Content that you make on your own
- Your interests as indicated by your interactions with organic content and advertisements.

Video information

While the user interaction signals are based on how you connect with other people while using the app, the video information signals are based on the content that you often look for while using the Discover tab.

This can include information such as:

- Captions
- Sounds
- Hashtags
- Effects
- Trending subjects

Device and account configurations

TikTok uses these variables to optimize performance. But since they are based on one-time settings choices instead of active engagements, they don't have as much of an effect on what you see on the platform as user interactions and video information signals.

The TikTok algorithm includes the following device and account settings:

- Language preference
- Place in the country (you may be more likely to see content from people in your own country)
- The type of mobile phone
- Categories of interest that you chose when you signed up

What is excluded from the TikTok algorithm?

The algorithm will NOT propose the following sorts of content:

- Duplicated content
- The content you've seen before Content that the algorithm identifies as spam
- Potentially distressing content (TikTok cites "graphic medical procedures" and "legal consumption of controlled commodities" as examples)

And here's some good news for new TikTok users or those who haven't yet amassed a significant following. TikTok does not make suggestions based on follower count or prior high-performing videos.

Yes, accounts with more followers are more likely to receive views since people are actively looking for such content. On the other hand, if you provide excellent content that is directed squarely at your target demographic, you have just as good of a chance of being featured on their For You page as an account that has previously had videos that have gone viral (this includes even the biggest TikTok stars).

Still not convinced? Here's the lowdown from TikTok:

"There are some videos on your feed that don't appear to have a large number of likes... You will have more possibilities to stumble onto new content categories, learn about new artists, and experience different perspectives if you include a variety of videos in your For You stream."

To reach your intended audience, you must become one of these up-and-coming creators. Here are ten pointers to get you started.

Tips For Working with The Tiktok Algorithm In 2022

Change to a business account

TikTok has two sorts of pro accounts based on whether you are a creator or a business. Although having a pro account will not help you get your videos on the For You page, switching to one is a crucial aspect of understanding the TikTok algorithm.

This is due to the fact that a Creator or Business account offers you access to analytics and insights that can help steer your TikTok strategy. If you want to generate content that your audience enjoys and engages with, you need to know who they are, when they use the app, and what type of content they appreciate.

Discover your subculture

It is critical to locate existing communities to connect with across all social networks. However, due to the nature of the TikTok algorithm, this is an even more critical stage for the app.

This is due to the fact that users of TikTok spend the majority of their time on the For You tab, in contrast to users of other social networks, where users spend the majority of their time connecting with accounts that they already follow.

If you can join a group or subculture that already exists, you're more likely to reach the right people. Fortunately, TikTok subcultures gravitate toward hashtags (more on those later).

Understanding your most valued subculture may also help you develop content that resonates with TikTokers in an authentic manner, hence enhancing your reputation, brand loyalty, and exposure.

TikTok has identified the following major subcultures:

#CottageCore For those who appreciate country cottages, gardens, and traditional aesthetics.

#MomsofTikTok For parenting tips and laughs.

#FitTok A place for fitness-related challenges, walkthroughs, and motivation.

Maximize the initial period

TikTok moves quickly. This isn't the place to introduce your video before getting into the heart of it. The hook of your video should entice people to stop scrolling.

In the early seconds of your TikTok, grab attention and demonstrate the worth of watching.

This statistic is from TikTok advertising, but it may be relevant to your original content as well: When you start a TikTok video with a strong emotion like surprise, it gets 1.7 times more views than when you start with a neutral expression.

Create an interesting caption

TikTok captions are limited to 150 characters, including hashtags. But that's no reason to ignore this magnificent real estate. A good caption should explain to readers why they should watch the video in question. This will boost the engagement and video completion rating signals that are sent to the algorithm.

Make use of your caption to generate interest or offer a question that will stimulate discussion among users in the comments.

Make high-quality videos just for TikTok

This should be self-evident, right? The For You page will not feature low-quality content.

You don't need any fancy gear to make authentic videos. In fact, your phone is the best tool you can use. To keep things going, you'll need good lighting, a good microphone, and a few shortcuts. TikToks can range in length from 5 seconds to 3 minutes, although 12 to 15 seconds is optimal for maintaining viewer interest.

You must shoot in the 9:16 vertical format. Vertically videoed videos have a 25% greater six-second watch-through rate. This makes it reasonable, given that they take up substantially more screen space.

Make sure the sound is on when you play your videos. Sound is "important" on TikTok, according to 88 percent of users. The tracks with the highest view-through rates are those that play at 120 beats per minute or above.

Also, make use of TikTok's built-in capabilities, including effects and text treatments. "These native features help your content feel like it belongs on the platform, which can help it show up on more For You pages," says TikTok.

Try out trending effects to see how they work with the TikTok algorithm. These are identified inside the effects menu of TikTok.

Post at the appropriate time for your audience

This is important on all social media sites, but it's especially important on TikTok. The algorithm takes into account the amount of time a user spends looking at your content

Check the stats of your Business or Creator account to determine the times of day during which your audience is the most engaged on the app:

- Tap the three-dot menu in the upper-right corner of your profile page.
- After selecting Business Suite, select Analytics.

TikTok recommends 1-4 daily posts.

Prioritize user-generated content

User-generated content (UGC) is any type of content (in this example, videos) made by TikTok users as opposed to brands. Prioritizing it is an effective method for fast gaining audience loyalty. This is because 56% of TikTok users feel like they know the brand better when it posts unpolished content about regular people.

UGC is so popular because it makes people feel like they're seeing something real. It's made by real customers who love your brand and want to show how great your products are without getting paid. Additionally, it has been found that customers are more willing to support a company that they have confidence in. Gen Z customers value authenticity, and in the past year, 63 percent of them have used TikTok once a week or more.

Encourage customers to tag you in their social media postings in order to generate positive user-generated content (UGC) for your brand. Be careful to verify the branded hashtag you've produced for your company for any user-generated that may have been tagged with it. Save user content you want to repost. Remember to give credit to the original creator when reposting UGC.

In addition to merely sharing previously created videos, consider replying to UGC with duets or stitching. You can respond to a Duet by slicing the screen in half, which will cause your response to playing alongside the video that was originally shown.

Stitch is a function that allows you to take segments of another video and use them on your own. So, if a client tags you in a video showcasing their latest purchase, you may combine a segment of their video with yours to create something altogether new.

UGC is also helpful because it can make up most of your content for the month. In the previous month, about 90 percent of the content was user-generated

Use the appropriate hashtags

There are two kinds of hashtags that can help your content rank higher in the TikTok algorithm:

Hashtags for the For You page

Tags such as #fyp and #foryou are frequently used in an attempt to climb to the top of the page for For You. TikTok won't say for sure if these work, but a lot of accounts use them, so it's worth a shot.

Trending hashtags

For the most up-to-date trends, click on the Discover page and press Trends.

Be on the lookout for hashtags associated with challenges. Hashtag challenges are a terrific method to generate new ideas for content while simultaneously sending the algorithm some positive emotions about trends.

Also, keep in mind: According to 61 percent of TikTokers, a brand's popularity increases when it participates in a TikTok craze.

Within the TikTok Creative Center, you also have the option to search for hashtags that are trending based on region. If you need inspiration, check out the top seven or 30-day trending TikToks by region.

Using TikTok's top small business hashtags, small businesses can tap into the network of individuals seeking to support independent companies.

TikTok for Business ✓
@TikTokBusiness

Small business conversations are already happening on TikTok—all you need to do is join in:

#smallbusiness – 33.8 billion views
#entrepreneur– 12.8 billion views
#smallbusinesscheck – 10.2 billion views
#sidehustle– 6.8 billion views
#supportsmallbusiness – 3.1 billion views

10:53 PM · Aug 11, 2021

♡ 4   ♡ Reply   & Copy link

Explore what's happening on Twitter

Use trending sounds and music

Music and sounds improve TikTok engagement and visibility. Here are some significant figures from recent investigations by MRC Data and Flamingo to demonstrate the point:

- 67% of people desire TikTok videos with trending audio
- 68% say trending audio helps them remember brands
- 58% of people are more likely to share a trending-sounds ad
- 62% are fascinated about the brand after viewing a trending sounds video

Incorporating popular music into your videos has obvious benefits. How can you identify popular TikTok sounds when trends change daily? Here's a quick way to find popular audio:

- Simply select Discover at the very bottom of the screen.

- You'll see a feed of all the hashtags and sounds that are popular across the app.

- Keep scrolling until you find an icon that looks like a music note enclosed in a circle on the left side of the screen. On the right, you'll see a number indicating how many TikTok videos use that sound.

You can also take a sound from someone else's video, as long as it's licensed for TikTok. Tap the spinning, round icon in the lower right corner of your screen to extract audio from a video.

You'll see a red button in the bottom-center of the screen that lets you browse through all of the videos that have that sound. Try this out.

Use analytics to keep track of engagement

You may acquire valuable insight into the types of content that your target audience enjoys seeing by monitoring the statistics of your TikTok for Business account and then incorporating that information into the creation of new and improved videos. The most significant advantage of adopting these KPIs is that they eliminate all guessing from your TikTok marketing plan.

TikTok's in-app metrics are classified into four types:

- Overview: Keeps track of engagement and follower count

- Content: Keeps track of your most popular videos.

- Followers: Audience growth and demographics are broken below.

- Live: Displays information from live videos.

Global data points, such as hashtag views and the Discover page, allow you to monitor trend performance over time. You'll be able to tell if a trend is still current and worth developing for. If "my coffee ritual" videos were extremely popular three months ago but are now barely seen, you know it's not a good idea to proceed.

THE COMPLETE TIKTOK ANALYTICS GUIDE: HOW TO ASSESS YOUR SUCCESS

When it comes to content strategy, TikTok analytics can help alleviate some of the uncertainty. Find out what your target audience is most interested in.

What metrics do you use to measure TikTok's success? There are a lot of things to look at, like the number of followers, likes, comments, and shares. But the data provided by TikTok go much further: they let you evaluate progress on a weekly and monthly basis, the total amount of video play time, information about who is watching, and plenty more.

Since there are more than 1 billion active TikTok accounts, every user has the chance to reach a huge audience, but not everyone does. That is why it is critical to review (and comprehend) your TikTok data. Track the correct data, and you'll be able to zero in on the strategies that are truly effective (and tell hype from reality).

If you're just getting started with TikTok marketing, analytics can eliminate some of the guesswork. When you have a TikTok Business account, you can get insights that can help you decide when and what to post.

Who has access to TikTok Analytics?

Anyone can. Or, more specifically, anyone with a TikTok Business account. These accounts, according to TikTok, provide "creative tools that empower corporations to think like marketers but act like creators." And the cost is reasonable (it's free).

How to Check Tiktok Analytics

On Mobile:

- Go to your profile

- In the top right corner, click the Settings and Privacy tab.
- Click the tab labeled Creator Tools located under Account.
- Choose Analytics from the drop-down menu.

On Desktop:

- Sign into TikTok.
- Hover your cursor over your profile photo in the upper right corner.
- Choose View Analytics.

You will need to use the desktop dashboard in order to download any of your analytics data. There is no other way to do this.

Classifications of TikTok Analytics

Analytics for Tiktok is broken up into four categories: Overview, Content, Followers, and Live.

Overview Analytics

On the Overview page, you have the option of viewing metrics for the most recent week, month, or two months; alternatively, you can select a date range of your own choosing.

Content analytics

This option will show you which of your videos have been seen the most times within a certain time frame that you choose. It also includes information about each post, such as views, likes, comments, and shares.

Follower analytics

The Follower tab displays information about your followers, such as gender breakdowns and where they're reading from. You may also monitor when your followers use the app the most.

Live Analytics

This category provides information about live videos you've hosted in the recent week or month (7 or 28 days). These data include your follower count, the amount of time you've spent live, and the number of Diamonds you've won.

What do the stats for TikTok Analytics Mean?

Overview tab metrics

The Overview tab provides a summary of the metrics listed below:

- **Video views.** How many times your videos were seen in a specific time period.
- **Profile views.** How many times your profile was looked at during the chosen time frame. This TikTok indicator is an excellent predictor of brand interest. It counts how many people liked your video enough to look at your profile or how many people are interested in what your brand is doing on the platform.
- **Likes.** The number of "likes" your videos got during the chosen time period.
- **Comments.** The total number of comments that were left on your videos within the timeframe that was selected.
- **Shares.** The amount of shares your videos obtained during the specified time period.
- **Followers**. The overall number of TikTok users who follow your account and how that has changed throughout the given time period.
- **Content.** The number of videos you've shared in the specified time frame.
- **LIVE.** The number of live videos you've hosted during the specified time period.

Content tab metrics

You can monitor the performance of your videos from the Content tab.

- **Trending videos.** Displays the top nine videos in terms of viewership increase over the last seven days.
- **Total video views.** The quantity of views a TikTok video has received.
- **Total like count of a post.** The number of likes a post has garnered.
- **Total number of comments.** The number of comments a post has generated.
- **Total number of shares.** The number of shares the post has received.
- **Total playtime.** A total of how long people have watched your video in total. The play time of a single post does not tell much on its own, but it may be compared to the performance of other posts to estimate your account's average total playtime.
- **Average watch time.** A rough estimate of how long viewers spend on average watching each of your videos. This will tell you a lot about how well you were able to keep people's attention.
- **Watched full video.** How many times the entire video has been viewed.
- **Reached audience.** The overall number of viewers of your video.
- **Video views by section.** Where your post's traffic is coming from. The For You feed, your profile, the Following feed, sounds, searches, and hashtags are all different types of traffic sources. If you're utilizing hashtags or noises to increase visibility, this is where you'll see how effective they were.
- **Video views by region.** This section reveals the top viewing locations for the post. This is how to tell if a post or marketing campaign you developed for a certain location was successful.

Followers tab metrics

To understand more about your audience, go to the Followers tab. You can examine your followers' interests in addition to vital audience demographic metrics, making this part a wonderful source of content ideas.

- **Gender.** The gender breakdown of your followers may be found here. If you're content with your niche, stick with it.
- **Top territories.** A country-by-country breakdown of your followers. Keep these locations in mind if you want to localize your content and promotions. The maximum number of countries listed here is five.
- **Follower activity.** This displays the times and days when your TikTok followers are most active. Look for times when activity is typically high and frequently post during that time period.
- **Videos your followers watched.** This area gives you an idea of the most popular content among your followers. Keep an eye on this section to see if it stimulates any content ideas. It's also a wonderful area to look for collaborators.
- **Sounds your followers listened to.** TikTok trends are frequently supported by audio tracks; therefore, you should check out the most popular sounds that your followers have listened to in order to determine what is trending. TikTok trends change quickly, so if you use these findings for inspiration, be prepared for a speedy turnaround.

If expanding your audience is one of your goals (and you want to see more activity on the Followers tab), you should think about producing that is more applicable to a wider audience. Alternately, you may think about engaging in influencer marketing and forming a partnership with a relevant creator in order to increase your visibility throughout a variety of communities.

LIVE tab metrics

The LIVE tab displays the following statistics for your live videos from the previous 7 or 28 days.

Total views. The total number of people who watched your live videos in the time range you chose.

Total time. The total amount of time you spent hosting live videos throughout the specified period range.

New followers. The number of new people who started following you while you were hosting a live video between the dates you chose.

Top viewer count. The maximum number of users who watched your live video at one time throughout the time span that was set.

Unique viewers. The total number of people who watched your live video at least once (Regarding this statistic, a viewer is only counted once, regardless of the number of times they rewatch the video).

Diamonds. When you broadcast a live video (and are 18 or older), viewers can send you virtual gifts such as "Diamonds." TikTok allows you to swap these gems for actual money.

Other TikTok Analytics

Hashtag views

This metric measures how many times a post with a certain hashtag has been seen.

To view the number of times a hashtag has been viewed, search for it in the Discover tab. The Top tab will display an overview of the search results. You'll be able to check the number of views, relevant hashtags, and some of the most popular videos that use the tag from there.

Total likes

You may view the total amount of likes you've received for all of your content on your TikTok profile. This TikTok measure could be utilized to get an idea of average engagement.

TikTok engagement rates

TikTok's engagement rates can be calculated in a number of various methods, just like those of other social media platforms. The two main formulas that marketers employ are as follows:

((Number of likes + Comments) / Number of Followers) * 100 or ((Number of likes + Comments + Shares) / Number of Followers) * 100

Because like and comment numbers are shown on the platform, you can readily compare your TikTok analytics to those of other accounts. Or, before collaborating with an influencer, research their engagement rates. This is simply one method for making money on TikTok (there are three more).

Average engagement estimate

Try the following for a rough estimate of an account's average engagement.

- Click Likes on a profile to view the complete number.
- Count how many videos have been posted.
- Divide the total number of likes by the total number of videos.
- Divide this figure by the total number of followers on the account.
- Multiply the result by 100.

Remember that most engagement rate algorithms incorporate comments in addition to likes, so don't compare our results to those. However, because counting overall comment totals takes time, this formula can be used to quickly compare accounts in-house.

INTRODUCTION TO TIKTOK ADVERTISING

How to Advertise on TikTok in 2022

TikTok marketing enables businesses to connect with younger, content-hungry demographics. If you follow these important tips, you can start making your own successful TikTok ads. If you still believe TikTok is only for kids, you're passing up a vital social media advertising opportunity for your company.

TikTok exceeded 1 billion users in September, and TikTok commercials can now reach an estimated 825 million adults (18+) worldwide.

Types of TikTok Advertising

Here are all of the many types of ads that can be run on TikTok's ad platform and its family of applications. Not all ad formats are offered everywhere. Further down in this post, you can see the TikTok ad requirements for all formats.

In-feed ads

These are self-service advertising that you may make using the TikTok Ad Manager interface.

TikTok's in-feed advertising is similar to the ads that appear between Instagram stories. When a person is scrolling through their feed, eventually, one of these advertisements will appear on the screen.

One of the best aspects of in-feed adverts is that they can be made virtually indistinguishable from regular if desired. However, if your strategy calls for it, you can add many CTAs and upload videos with elaborate motion graphics. Overall, they give us a great deal of flexibility.

To launch an in-feed marketing campaign on TikTok for business, you must invest at least $500. These TikTok ads are the least expensive of all the different kinds.

TopView Ads

TopViews are a specialized form of in-feed advertisement; after a user has scrolled for three seconds, the user is certain to view a TopView before any other in-feed advertisement. They also appear at the top of the For You page and are capable of supporting full-screen video for up to sixty seconds at a time.

Image ads

These advertisements comprise an image, the company or app name, and ad text, and they are exclusively available in the TikTok News Feed applications (BuzzVideo, TopBuzz, and Babe).

Video ads

Video advertisements are available for TikTok or the TikTok family of news applications. They show up in the user's For You feed as 5–60 second full-screen videos. Each advertisement consists of a video, a display image, the name of the brand or application, and ad text.

Spark ads

Advertisers can use Spark Ads to boost their own or other people's organic content on their accounts. According to TikTok data, regular In-Feed advertising have a 142 percent lower engagement rate and a 24 percent lower completion rate than Spark Ads.

Pangle ads

Advertisements placed via the TikTok Audience Network.

Carousel ads

These are only available in TikTok's News Feed applications and include up to ten photos with distinct captions in each ad.

Tiktok Advertisements Formats for Brands

Managed brands are those that collaborate with a TikTok sales representative to promote their products. They get access to more ad formats, such as:

Branded Hashtag Challenge

A framework for an advertising campaign that lasts between three and six days and encourages involvement by displaying user-generated content on the page dedicated to the hashtag challenge.

Using user-generated , branded hashtag challenges boost brand recognition (UGC).

These challenges are displayed on the Discover tab of TikTok. When visitors click on one of the hashtags, they are taken to a branded landing page that gives information about the challenge, a link to the brand's website, and user-generated content from previous participants in the challenge.

Branded hashtag challenges are particularly effective because, well, they're fun. In contrast to in-feed advertisements or brand takeovers, these ads allow users to be creative and express themselves, resulting in a valuable relationship between your business and your audience.

Unfortunately, these advertisements are also highly costly. For a six-day challenge, you must pay a flat price of $150,000.

Branded Effects

Stickers, filters, and special effects with your brand's name on them can encourage users to interact with your brand on TikTok. TikTok's branded effects follow in Snapchat's footsteps by allowing advertisers to develop AR overlays that TikTokers may utilize in their videos.

These, like branded hashtag challenges, can be successful because they stimulate audience participation. They are, however, rather pricey, with each effect costing $100,000.

How To Set Up a Tiktok Ad Campaign

Simply visit TikTok Ads Manager to create a TikTok advertising campaign. In order to proceed, you'll first need to sign up for TikTok Ads Manager.

You do not require an Ads Manager account if you are only wanting to boost existing content. TikTok Promote is an alternative.

Choose your goal.

To begin, log in to TikTok Ads Manager and select the **Campaign** option. TikTok has seven advertising goals divided into three categories:

1. **Awareness**

    a. **Reach**: Get as many people as possible to see your ad (in beta).

2. **Consideration**

    a. **Traffic**: Drive visitors to a specified URL.

    b. **App Installs**: Get people to download your application.

    c. **Video Views**: Increase video ad playtime (in beta).

    d. **Lead Generation**: Use an Instant Form that is already filled out to get leads.

    e. **Conversions**

3. **Conversions**: Get people to do certain things on your site, like make a purchase or sign up for a service.

    a. **Catalog Sales**: Ads that change based on what you sell (in beta and only available to those with a managed ad account in supported regions).

Set a budget and give your campaign a name

The name of your campaign should be easy to remember for everyone on your team. It can have a maximum of 512 characters.

If you have unlimited funds or prefer to establish budget limits for individual ad groups rather than the entire campaign, you can set your campaign budget to No Limit. Otherwise, decide whether your campaign's budget will be daily or lifetime (more on that below).

Campaign budget optimization is also achievable by utilizing the Lowest Cost bidding approach for the App Installs and Conversions targets.

TikTok is beta-testing a function that suggests a bid in order to optimize Cost Per Click goals.

Choose an ad group name, then select ad locations

Each campaign has between one and 999 ad groups. Each ad group can have a name of up to 512 characters.

For each ad group, you can select a different location. Not all positions are available in every location:

- **TikTok placement**: Ads that appear within the For You stream.

- **News Feed App placement**: There are advertisements contained throughout TikTok's other applications, such as BuzzVideo, TopBuzz, NewsRepublic, and Babe.

- **Pangle placement**: The TikTok audience network.

- **Automatic placement** enables TikTok to automate the optimization of ad delivery.

Select whether to employ Automated Creative Optimization

You will not be able to upload your creative until you reach the stage of producing individual adverts. You can choose whether or not to let TikTok automatically combine your images, videos, and ad text for the time being. The best-performing ads will then be shown by the ad system.

TikTok suggests that new marketers enable this feature.

Choose your audience carefully

TikTok, like other social ads, allows you to tailor your adverts to a certain demographic. You can utilize a lookalike or bespoke audience, or you can target your ads based on demographics.:

- Gender

- Age

- Location

- Language

- Interests

- Behaviors

- Device details

Set a budget and a schedule for your ad groups

You have already established a budget for the entire campaign. Now is the moment to establish the advertising group's budget and timetable.

After deciding whether you want your ad group to have a daily or lifetime budget, pick the beginning and ending times for it. You may also select to run your ad at particular times throughout the day under Dayparting (based on your account time zone).

Determine your bidding strategy and optimize it

First, decide whether you want to optimize for conversions, clicks, or reach. This target may be determined automatically by your campaign objective.

Next, decide on your bidding strategy.

- Bid Cap: The maximum amount paid per click (CPC), view (CPV), or 1,000 impressions (CPM).

- Cost Cap: A cost per result average for optimum CPM. The cost may go higher or lower than the amount that was bid, but it should normalize to the amount that was offered.

- Lowest Cost: The ad system employs the ad group budget to produce the greatest number of results at the lowest cost per result.

Finally, decide if you want standard or fast delivery. Standard allocates your spending evenly over the campaign's specified days, whereas rapid delivery spends your budget as quickly as possible.

Set up your ad(s)

Each ad group has 20 adverts. Each ad name, which is only intended for internal usage, can be up to 512 characters long (it does not appear on the ad itself).

To begin, select your ad format: picture, video, or Spark ad. If you're only going to use TikTok itself and not any of the other applications in the TikTok family, your only advertising options are video or Spark ads.

Add photographs or video, or make a video with Ads Manager's video template or tools. TikTok research suggests that the video editor can reduce CPA by 46%.

Select one of the preset thumbnails or upload your own. Then type in your text and link. Examine the ad preview on the right side of the screen, then add any applicable tracking links and hit Submit.

Your ad will be reviewed before it is published.

To use Spark Ads, you must first contact the creators of the content you wish to use and request an access code.

TikTok Promote

TikTok Promote can also be used to boost existing content. Anyone above the age of 18 can use TikTok Promote to promote current content. It's TikTok's version of Facebook Boost.

To give a TikTok a boost, do the following:

1. Tap the three-line symbol for settings on your TikTok profile, then tap Creator tools.

2. Select Promote.

3. Select the video that you want to promote.

4. Pick one of these three objectives for your advertising campaign: more views of your videos, more visits to your website, or more followers.

5. Choose your target audience, budget, and length of time, and then tap Next.

6. Enter your payment information and then click Start Promotion.

TikTok Ad Specs

In this part, we'll concentrate on ads that appear on TikTok rather than the TikTok family applications.

TikTok video ad specs

- Aspect ratio: 9:16, 1:1, or 16:9. The most successful videos are those that are vertical and have a ratio of 9:16.

- 540 x 960 px or 640 x 640 px is the minimum resolution. Videos with 720 px resolution perform best.

- File formats include mp4,.mov,.mpeg,.3gp, and.avi.
- Duration: 5-60 seconds. TikTok suggests 21-34 seconds for optimal performance.
- Max file size: 500 MB
- Profile image: a square image that is less than 50 KB in size.
- Name of the app or brand: 2-20 characters or 4-40 characters (app) (brand)
- Ad description: 1-100 characters, and no emojis

Spark ad specs

- Aspect ratio: Any
- Minimum resolution: Any
- Duration: Any
- Max file size: Any
- Account mentions and emojis permitted
- The display name and text are based on the original organic post's content.

Note: The character count is calculated using Latin characters. The character count for Asian characters is usually half.

How Much do TikTok Ads Cost?

Minimum budgets

TikTok advertisements are bid-based. You have the ability to keep expenditures under control by setting daily and lifetime budgets for ad groups and campaigns. The minimal budgets are as follows:

Campaign level

- Daily budget: $50
- Lifetime budget: $50

Ad group level

- Daily budget: $20

- The lifetime budget is determined by multiplying the daily budget by the total number of days planned for the event.

TikTok does not disclose precise ad costs, but they do provide the following advice and insights:

- If you are going to be employing a Bid Cap or Cost Cap bidding approach, make sure that your initial campaign-level budget is set to "No Limit" and that your daily ad group budget is at least 20 times higher than your desired cost per action (CPA).

- When setting up your initial budget for app event optimization, you should aim for at least $100 or 20 times your target (CPA), whichever is higher.

- Set an initial budget for your Conversions campaign of at least $100 or 20 times your target (CPA), whichever is larger. If you are utilizing the Lowest Cost bid method, this money should be used.

TikTok Ads Cost Examples

TikTok also discloses the expenditures associated with a number of specific campaigns, which can serve as a useful comparison for your own spending:

- Synth Labs International, a company that makes skin care products, ran a Spark Ads campaign to get 300,000 impressions at $0.32 CPC.

- Lion Wild, an online jewelry store, employed video advertisements to produce a 19.35 percent conversion rate at $0.13 CPC and $0.17 CPM.

- G2A, an online gaming marketplace, achieved 12 million impressions with video advertisements at $0.16 CPM and $0.06 CPC.

- Playa Games, a mobile game publisher, used video ads to get a 130 percent return on ad expenditure with a €0.06 CPC.

- TVNZ OnDemand, a BVOD streaming service, got a 0.5 percent click-through rate at NZ$0.42 CPC.

- Mallows Beauty achieved a 2.86 percent click-through rate at £0.04 CPC.

- Strike Gently Co. used TikTok Promote to achieve a 1.9 percent click-through rate at $0.27 CPC.

- Hyundai Australia employed video advertisements to achieve a 0.88 percent click-through rate at a cost-per-click (CPC) of less than $0.30.

The expenses of TikTok advertisements are subject to sales tax if that tax is required in your area. Only marketers based in Hawaii must pay sales tax in the United States (4.71 percent). VAT of 20% is charged to UK marketers. This amount is added to the total amount you spend on ads, so be aware that tax will be added to your bill.

TikTok Advertising Best Practices

Combine and contrast your creative styles

Rather than using the same or extremely comparable creatives, vary your approach. To combat audience fatigue, TikTok recommends refreshing your creative every seven days.

Change it up inside each video as well. TikTok suggests using different scenes with B-roll or transition .

Cut to the chase

TikTok suggests keeping video advertisements between 21 and 34 seconds in length.

To avoid losing viewers, make the opening 3 to 10 seconds very eye-catching and interesting. The finest TikTok ads highlight the main message or product inside the first three seconds.

Use both sound and captions

Audio is used in 93 percent of the top-performing TikTok videos, and 73 percent of TikTok users stated they would stop and look at commercials with audio.

Tracks that clock in at more than 120 beats per minute is typically the most popular.

However, captions and text are also significant. Use words to emphasize your call to action in particular. TikTok discovered that text overlays appear in 40% of auction ads with the greatest view-through rate.

Maintain your positivity and authenticity

TikTok advises users to keep their videos "positive, sincere, and motivating." This is neither the place to try out your that is dark and moody nor is it the place to utilize a hard-sell approach to make a sale. You also don't want a video that appears overly "made."

To keep your adverts truly authentic, try using user-generated . One in every three of the top auction advertising, for example, features someone looking straight at the camera and speaking to the viewer.

Royal Essence, an Australian company, employed a similar method to get 2.2 million impressions and 50,000 clicks.

HOW TO GO VIRAL ON TIKTOK

On TikTok, going viral does not depend on the number of followers a user has. Learn how to make your content stand out.

TikTok isn't just for dancing teenagers anymore. The platform has evolved into one of today's most dynamic social media communities. It is also one of the few social media networks that make it easy to go viral.

Anyone may go viral on TikTok, whether they have 2 or 200K followers. It's not by chance. The app's algorithm gives all users an equal chance to go viral and create an audience over time. It's a rare case of social media meritocracy.

However, despite the fact that TikTok levels the playing field for its users, this does not mean that there are no actions that can be taken to increase the likelihood of a video going viral.

How Does Tiktok Content Go Viral?

TikTok's algorithm, like the algorithms used by other social media platforms, recommends videos to its users that are similar to the videos they have already watched and interacted with.

The recommendation algorithm of the site examines the videos that users have viewed, liked, shared, and commented on. It then breaks down characteristics such as the video content, the text that is utilized in the video, and the background music. It then shows them similar content from other TikTok users that they may not already be following. This is posted to the FYP (or For You Page) feed.

Consider it like channel surfing, except you have a different cable bundle every time you turn on the TV.

The TikTok algorithm does not take into account a TikTok profile's following count or historical engagement levels. You're just as likely to see a million-view post as a video from a brand-new user.

Furthermore, every TikTok video has the potential to go viral via the For You tab. When you post a video, the app displays it on the FYP of a tiny handpicked group of users. Depending on how well it performs there, it may be promoted to a bigger audience.

Not every video will land this way, but this TikTok algorithm function provides every upload the opportunity to make an impact.

Nine Tips to Go Viral on Tiktok

Even while TikTok is largely a democratic platform, there are still opportunities to publish content that has the potential to go viral. In point of fact, one of the most effective strategies for making a post go viral on the app is frequently just to engage with the TikTok community in a realistic manner.

Understand trends

It is simple to comprehend the rationale behind TikTok's first success with a more youthful demographic. It is fiercely trend-driven, bringing memes and video formats to the forefront. The next great phenomenon may sweep over in a matter of days, but every meme has its time.

You don't have to search far for a trend to follow. In fact, you're probably looking at one right now on your For You page.

TikTok trends frequently behave similarly to Mad Libs. There will be trending audio, a dance, and a text-based format to which people can add their own flavor. They can stay for months, although they usually only stay for a few days. They come and go rapidly, but when they do, they're an excellent method to get your work in front of a larger audience.

Because of the way the algorithm is designed, the promotion of videos that are relevant to a trend within the app increases in proportion to the number of people who engage with the trend. As a result, what is the first step to getting viral on TikTok? Keep a watch on those trends, you guessed it. The more current you are with TikTok content trends, the easier it will be to develop relevant and timely .

Make use of humor

TikTok's primary currency is humor, which is not surprising given that comedy is an integral aspect of any social media platform. Humor is the common thread that runs across all of these different types of videos, from lifestyle vlogging to workout motivation.

Every TikTok community, especially the more serious ones, provides an opportunity for members to demonstrate their sense of humor.

Users are more inclined to watch an entire video if it has humor. If people discover that you share their sense of humor, they may even subscribe to your videos in the long run.

On TikTok, you don't have to be the next big thing on SNL to make people laugh. As cheesy as it may sound, they will respond best if you are yourself.

You should feel comfortable using hashtags

TikTok's algorithm takes into account hashtags as one of its ranking signals. This indicates that using hashtags in your video description makes it simple for the algorithm to place it in front of the audience that is most likely to respond to it.

Showing off your latest makeup haul? Include the hashtags #makeup and #MUA. Creating content for a popular show? Include a relevant hashtag (such as #SquidGame) to help TikTok promote your videos to fans.

Avoid using merely generic hashtags such as #FYP. By doing this, you will avoid having to go up against the countless other videos using the same hashtag.

In terms of quantity, three to five hashtags per post are usually more than enough to get the suggestion system started. If you use too many, the system may not know to who to expose your .

Make it short

There are three distinct time constraints for videos that can be uploaded to TikTok: 15 seconds, 60 seconds, and 3 minutes. There is nothing preventing you from using the whole one minute and eighty seconds.

Nonetheless, brevity is the soul of wit (Shakespeare said so, so you know it's true). And the app that TikTok most successfully imitates isn't YouTube. It's the now-defunct Vine, which had a video duration limit of six seconds. That may not sound like much, but consider it some of the greatest Vines of all time. Would it be better for any of them to be longer? Most likely not.

A brief video does not allow the spectator to lose interest. When the autoplay feature starts, it does give them more time to go back and watch it again. Because of this, people tend to watch and interact with short videos more.

In addition, there is a good probability that you are not simply cleverly increasing the number of people who watch your movie by keeping the length of its running duration on the shorter side. Your content's creative quality is also improving.

Encourage participation

Interactivity distinguishes a video platform from a social network. TikTok is more than just a video-sharing app. It's also a place to interact with a community about the stuff it produces. There's a reason for a comment section, you know? Furthermore, the Duet and Stitch capabilities allow you to work on videos with complete strangers on the other side of the world.

TikTok's algorithm rewards all types of community participation, so make sure your encourages it. Request that users respond in the comments section, and then provide a prompt from which they can Stitch or Duet their own reaction video. Create videos that viewers feel motivated to share on other social media channels, such as Instagram. It all contributes to the algorithm favorably seeing your content.

Recognize your target audience

There's a lot going on TikTok these days. It's home to a plethora of communities centered on everything from health to emo music. These communities are extremely supportive of one another.

While you are not required to adhere to one subject, it is beneficial to concentrate on one specialized area of competence or interest. The more often your content appears in a certain community, the easier it is to gain a following. This may result in increased views from a core audience and an improvement in the video's performance on the For You page.

Understanding your target demographic will also assist you in determining the optimum times to post on TikTok. While determining the optimum time to post won't necessarily make you go viral overnight, it will help get your content in front of more people - which is a good place to start.

Use the TikTok tools

TikTok's video editing features do not stop with your camera. The app has a large collection of popular songs and audio clips. Users can also choose from a variety of entertaining video effects. You don't need a video degree to create amazing videos with this software. The platform offers you all of the necessary tools.

This is beneficial in two ways. For one reason, a distinct and distinctive style of video creation can aid in the development of an audience. Using popular sounds and filters also works to your advantage. Users who have previously engaged with those unique sounds and effects will be more likely to see your videos.

Be discreetly controversial

An excellent approach to get people interested in any platform? Say something that will engross (or anger or amuse) them to the point where they will have no choice but to reply.

We're not saying you should cross any red lines. The easiest way to court controversy is to simply state that you did not enjoy the most recent album by Drake or the most critically praised superhero movie.

Hot takes are one of the driving factors behind social media nowadays, and TikTok is no exception. They can produce a lot of engagement for your TikTok account, even if it gets a little hot.

Take a step back

TikTok is vying for your attention. If you leave it after publishing a video, it will try to entice you to return. It does this by attempting to generate notifications, and the simplest way for it to do so is to show your movie to more people. After you've uploaded a video to TikTok, the best thing you can do is wait a little while before opening it up again so you can check the number of views your video has received in real-time. It is possible that when you return, you will find a deluge of new views, comments, and shares.

IDEAS TO GET YOUR SMALL BUSINESS STARTED ON TIKTOK

TikTok marketing has rapidly evolved to become one of the most effective methods for showcasing your company in the realm of social media.

The one-minute video app claimed to have more than one billion monthly active users and to have been the most downloaded app in 2020 in 2021.

TikTok is well-known for memes, dancing challenges, and viral moments; in addition, the platform has attracted a variety of businesses, including both large and small enterprises. In fact, it's difficult to find top sellers who aren't at least dabbling with the app.

If you're new to TikTok, it can be intimidating to begin using an entirely new platform, especially one that has its own peculiarities, trends, and filters.

Why Should Businesses Post on Tiktok?

We have proven, however, that TikTok is quite popular, but does this mean that it will genuinely assist people in learning about your brand?

The answer is an emphatical yes. TikTok, in contrast to many other social media networks, does not restrict the videos it shows you to those posted by users you already follow. The For You page of the app is a never-ending stream of content that includes a good dose of videos from people you don't follow but who the app thinks you would like based on your viewing history and preferences. This indicates that there is a good chance that prospective clients will discover your videos without visiting your profile first.

TikTok constantly updates the app with new videos in an effort to keep users there as long as possible. Therefore, if you sell cosmetics, for instance, TikTok aims to place your content in front of beauty fans.

TikTok may do wonders for your company, but the trick is generating content people genuinely want to watch, favorite, and share.

Because of this novel approach to discoverability, accounts have the potential to become overnight viral phenomena, and the rate at which brands that put out content can expand has increased exponentially.

On the app, there is even a group dedicated to entrepreneurs called #smallbusiness. Members of this community share and promote using their own sounds, trends, and hashtags.

Customers will be brought straight to your establishment if you take advantage of the free business account that TikTok offers and include the URL of your online store in your profile bio. You can also include a Linkpop page, which enables you to curate your online store, featured products, and other forms of information with a single link.

TikTok may do wonders for your brand, but the key is to create content that people want to watch, favorite, and share.

8 Tiktok Ideas You Can Use for Your Small Business

Behind the scenes

One of the most common and well-received types of videos that businesses upload to TikTok is one that takes viewers behind the scenes of their operations.

Customers now get an inside peek at how their orders are processed thanks to these TikTok videos, which demonstrate the realities of running a business.

People want to see evidence of what you're doing, whether you're shipping your first order or discussing your launch day sales.

That doesn't mean you have to go into exhaustive detail, but demonstrating how you manage your firm adds a human element and satisfies curiosity. You'd be surprised what individuals find interesting that you might just pass by on your way to work.

Regardless of where you are in the process, there is always something interesting to discuss.

You may also try making a TikTok video of:

- Arranging your merchandise or office space

- Celebrating landmarks such as 100 sales or an anniversary
- Preparing for the launch of a new product
- Demonstrating how you develop and choose products

Pack an order

Putting a video of you packing orders is a fun way to show what goes on behind the scenes and how much care you put into each order.

This is your opportunity to demonstrate to potential clients what to expect when their product comes. It's a particularly good idea if you include freebies, thank-you cards, or special packaging.

Some TikTok businesses have customers who want to watch their order package in a video, which is an added incentive for them if you have time. Just remember not to give any sensitive information about a customer, such as their entire name or address.

Business advise and tips

Many other small company owners and prospective entrepreneurs on TikTok would appreciate your guidance, which you can share. While such advice may entice them, they can also become customers and help you develop your following so that even more people see your TikToks.

Again, you don't have to tell everyone everything, but being honest makes you seem more real. In the process, you will also develop your reputation as a company leader and an inspiration to others.

You could tell:

- How to successfully introduce a new product
- How to Locate a Manufacturer
- What actions you do (and don't take!)
- The most effective marketing channels

Some are lengthier series of suggestions, while others are short videos with catchy music and inspirational snippets. Remember that TikTok is not LinkedIn. There should be some form of amusement.

Show how people use your products

You shouldn't only post this kind of TikTok, but you should definitely show off your goods or services.

This is best accomplished by displaying your products in use. What you show depends on the product you're selling, but here are some ideas:

- Displaying a product's water or weather resistance
- displaying the stretchiness of your fabric
- Instructions for applying a skin care product
- A video demonstrating a candle's burn time.
- jewelry and clothing pairing
- making a makeup appearance
- Using a handcrafted mug
- Using your own utensils or cookware

This approach will enable the public to see and comprehend how your product will fit into their life.

New product launches

By teasing new products on TikTok, you may generate buzz before they are ever released. This prepares clients to buy when the product becomes available and also demonstrates your ability to expand your brand.

This is an excellent opportunity to highlight what makes your products distinctive, generate demand for them, and discuss how you're responding to what your customers want.

You could even use these in a countdown series leading up to launch day to increase anticipation.

Learn about yourself or your employees

TikTok is a social media app that is driven by individuals and personalities. The mainstay of the app is TikToks of users merely conversing with the camera, but you don't need to possess the glitzy charisma of a full-time influencer to succeed in this format.

People enjoy getting to know the person behind a brand in order to provide a human factor. It's also considerably more fascinating to watch a person rather than a continuous stream of things.

This can be difficult if you're not used to being on camera, but it will grow simpler as you become more familiar with the app.

To begin, post a basic "get to know me" TikTok and discuss why you began your business.

Interact with clients

TikTok's capabilities encourage involvement in a variety of ways.

The first category is duets. If you turn this option on, you can make a TikTok that has a video from someone else next to it. This is a fun way to respond to customers who make videos of their orders or reviews of your products. You may also encourage viewers to share these movies by providing discount codes.

Another option is to make a video out of a comment. You have the option of clicking the "Reply" button and videoing a video that includes an overlay of the customer's message if they pose a question or offer you positive feedback.

Interacting with customers makes them feel acknowledged and valued, and it also provides you with another choice for providing . This is true regardless of the context.

Look for a pattern

If you're stuck for ideas, TikTok is always full of trending sounds, memes, and challenges.

To determine what content is currently popular on TikTok, you will need to devote some of your time to browse the platform. Following the accounts of other companies in order to gain inspiration from the content that they provide is a fantastic idea.

Because people will be hunting for that particular sound or meme, jumping on a trend is another smart approach to generate traction for a video because people will be searching for it.

Go forth and create some TikTok magic

You should now have a few suggestions for getting started on TikTok or reactivating your account. Even with just these eight suggestions, you'll be well on your way to publishing frequently because each format may be applied in a variety of ways.

TikTok can be temperamental, so knowing when to post on TikTok is critical. Some movies will be successful, while others will not; you must continue to attempt new ideas and experiment. You never know when you'll hit the big time.

HOW TO MAKE MONEY ON TIKTOK IN 2022

Perhaps it is your entrepreneurial spirit. Perhaps you've heard of Addison Rae, a 21-year-old driver of a Tesla Model X. Possibly, after seeing the "screen time" warning (the one in which your phone subtly reminds you that you are addicted to the internet), you thought to yourself, "Hey, might as well monetize this."

Regardless of how you arrived, you are quite welcome. To generate money on TikTok, here are the steps you need to take.

As of January 2022, more than 1 billion people were using TikTok. This made it the sixth most popular social media site in the world. That's a large market.

There are a lot of people who have already discovered how to make money on TikTok, and some of them even consider it to be their full-time profession. Here are some of the most effective methods for earning money with the app.

Is It Possible to Profit from Tiktok?

Yes, it is possible to earn money with TikTok.

But you have to be creative to make money on TikTok, just like when you paint a picture or try to figure out if your ex's ex is in a relationship. There are numerous more ways to generate money on the platform—even if you don't have a large following—in addition to the official, app-funded methods of making money (see Strategy #4 below).

Many users of the TikTok app have already achieved financial success through the use of the platform, much like social media creators who are active on other platforms. While TikTok may appear to be a fresh frontier, the tactics you might employ to make money are likely to be old.

How Much Will TikTokers Earn in 2022?

There are numerous ways to generate money on TikTok, and your revenue will be determined by how you monetize your account.

TikTok brand deals can earn you up to $80,000 per month. That's right; if you're a successful creator on the platform with a sizable and engaged following, you can use the money from one video to purchase a luxury vehicle.

You have the potential to earn between 2 and 4 cents through the TikTok Creator Fund for every 1,000 views that your videos receive. This means that after a million views, you may expect to earn $20 to $40.

How to Make Money on TikTok in 2022

Get money from TikTok's Creator Fund

This is the app-approved moneymaking strategy we discussed previously. TikTok announced its new Creator Fund on July 22, 2020, giving $200 million USD to "support those who dream of leveraging their voices and creativity to spark remarkable professions."

The internet ate it up, and a week later, they announced that the fund would grow to $1 billion USD by 2023. So, how do you obtain that enticing creator cash? Before you may apply, you must check the following boxes on the app:

- Be located in the United States, the United Kingdom, France, Germany, Spain, or Italy

- You must be at least 18 years old.

- Have a minimum of 10,000 followers.

- Have received at least 100,000 video views in the previous 30 days

- Keep to the guidelines and conditions of service set forth by the TikTok community.

As long as you have TikTok Pro, you can apply for the Creator Fund using the app.

Sell your own stuff

TikTok is an excellent platform for monetizing almost any type of video. Any creator, whether a dancer, musician, or comedian, can create and sell apparel to their most devoted fans.

And, with so many print-on-demand firms to choose from, there are a plethora of items to choose from. T-shirts, tote bags, pillow covers, hats, coffee cups, stickers, notebooks—or any combination of products—could be sold.

Profitability is not the only advantage of selling print-on-demand products. Owning branded merchandise provides your fans with a more personal connection to your work, and each follower who wears your stuff in public presents a fresh opportunity to spread the word about your brand wherever they go.

If you already have a product line or are thinking about starting one, TikTok can help you market it. With a TikTok for Business account, creators in the United States, Canada, or the United Kingdom can add a shopping tab and product links to their profiles.

Due to TikTok's collaboration with Shopify and other e-commerce platforms, the shopping tab has been added as a new feature. It is geared toward assisting TikTokers who already have a Shopify store in promoting their wares within the TikTok app. Users who click on a product link are taken to the merchant's Shopify site to make a purchase.

Brands such as Youth to the People and Glow Recipe, about which TikTok has released a case study, have taken use of the Shop option on the app by making their actual items available for sale and buying within the app. This feature is currently only available in the United States and the United Kingdom, which is an important consideration for enterprises outside of those nations.

One of the drawbacks of utilizing TikTok Shopping is that TikTok Business accounts can only access generic sounds. This makes it more challenging to engage in trends on the app, so you'll need to come up with some innovative solutions to this problem. An intriguing illustration of this may be seen in a video that went viral in which the social media manager for Bed, Bath and Beyond hummed a viral sound that the company was unable to access due to restrictions placed on Business accounts.

Partner with a reputable brand

TikTok defines sponsored content as in exchange for which you receive anything of value. Isn't that the goal? For example, a brand may pay you to make a TikTok video about how wonderful their soy candles smell, or you may be given a free skydiving vacation in exchange for writing about it. (However, we do not encourage taking advantage of any free skydiving offers.)

And brands are eager to participate in such compensated collaborations. According to a survey on influencer marketing, in December 2019, 16 percent of US marketers expected to employ TikTok for influencer campaigns—but by March 2021, that percentage had risen to 68 percent. To put it another way, influencer marketing is exploding on the platform.

Companies want to partner with people who have a following that knows and trusts them, according to the same eMarketer report, especially in the light of the COVID-19 pandemic and ongoing social justice campaigns.

This brings us to an essential point: don't seek out partnerships with companies whose viewpoints differ from yours. You alone determine how you interact with your audience. Your followers may be interested in the illuminating soup metaphors you share with them, the number of languages you can communicate in, or the number of manicures you can perform, but they are also interested in your ethics.

Here are some pointers to help you get started with sponsored content:

Only contact brands or organizations that you truly admire

If everything on your TikTok is about your transition to raw veganism, and then all of a sudden, you start posting about your favorite burger spot in town, your fans are going to be able to see right through you. This is not only unclear, but it also makes you appear to be a sellout. As a result, ensure that your sponsored is consistent with your overall culture.

Create a press kit for your TikTok channel

A press kit is similar to a personal movie trailer. It promotes all of your wonderful qualities (and gives brands good reasons to partner with you) and includes contact information, images, and notable accomplishments. Make them eager to see what happens next while holding a bag of popcorn. Templates for press kits are available for free on websites such as Templatelab.

Make a few unsponsored posts

It is imperative that you demonstrate to brands that you have the ability to increase revenue for their company. You can increase the likelihood that a specialized sock manufacturer will want to collaborate with you by publishing a few posts on social media that are not sponsored and in which you discuss your favorite pair of shoes.

Toggle the Branded Content switch

People dislike being duped, and it turns out that applications dislike it as well. TikTok developed the Branded Content option to ensure that users were being honest. If you're working on content for sponsorships, click the button (or risk your video being taken down).

Collaboration with an influencer

This method is the inverse of the last one. Reach out to an influencer on TikTok whose content is congruent with your brand if you run an established company that wants to expand its presence on the platform in order to generate more revenue.

According to this Tomoson analysis, every dollar spent on influencer marketing returned an average of $6.50 to the business, with the top 13% claiming a return of $20. Furthermore, half of the marketers believe that clients acquired through influencer marketing are of greater quality than customers acquired through other channels such as email marketing or organic search.

Finally, influencers, well, influence. Effectively. (Including micro-influencers!)

If you live in the United States, TikTok Creator Marketplace can help you identify the ideal influencer for you. The marketplace portal brings companies and influencers together. Any brand can join, but influencers can only join via invitation (for now).

Outside of the United States and the TikTok-approved marketplace, look for hashtags related to you and your business (#dentist, #faintinggoats, #thrifting) and skim through the . Alternatively, you may just explore the app by liking the videos you enjoy and dismissing (or clicking "Not interested") the ones you don't. The app will begin to display what you have requested. It's frighteningly intelligent in that way.

Examine each creator's page carefully—we've all heard the age-old story of the sobbing influencer's non-racism, non-apology. Steer clear of troublesome TikTokers. It's 2022.

Collect donations from supporters to crowdfund initiatives

For creators who are interested in making actual money, one of the most accessible paths to pursue is crowdfunding. You put in a lot of time and effort to create for your followers, so providing an easy, no-pressure way for them to give back is ideal for maintaining a consistent source of cash.

Depending on the type of cash you want, crowdfunding can take several forms. If you need startup cash for a certain project, you can rally your supporters by establishing a funding target and holding live fundraising events.

If you wish to sponsor a specific project, consider the following crowdfunding sites:

Kickstarter. Because Kickstarter is the most popular crowdfunding platform on the internet, its largest value is the number of supporters and brand awareness.

Indiegogo. If you don't have a specified financial goal, Indiegogo may be a better option because it allows you to receive funds after the deadline.

Fundable. Fundable allows entrepreneurs to trade shares for money, making it an excellent tool for locating investors. Fundable, on the other hand, is now exclusively available to residents of the United States.

Crowdcube. Crowdcube's Crowdcube Funded Club provides firms that meet their fundraising goals with exclusive perks from its partner organizations.

Crowdfunder. Crowdfunder allows businesses to raise financing from authorized investors by connecting them with a network of over 12,000 venture capitalists and angel investors.

Mighty Cause. Mighty Cause's simple platform is ideal for quickly developing a funding page to collect donations because there are no fees or waiting periods for approvals before launching your campaign.

SeedInvest. SeedInvest allows non-accredited investors to invest in enterprises through their websites. Your backers on SeedInvest are investors rather than supporters; therefore, funds are donated in exchange for shares.

Ask your audience for "tips."

Crowdfunding platforms may not be the best option if you don't have a specific project in mind or aren't ready to give equity to investors. Consider employing a tipping platform to receive donations quickly and easily.

Tipping platforms provide a more intimate financial choice. They function exactly like a traditional tip jar. Fans have the opportunity to contribute, but doing so is in no way required, and they are free to do so whenever and in whatever amount they see fit.

If this appeals to you, here are some excellent tipping sites to consider:

Tipeee. Tipeee does not provide subscription services, but its power is in its simplicity. Tipeee allows authors to build up a page where their admirers can directly "tip" them any amount they want, whenever they want.

Buy Me a Coffee. Buy Me a Coffee takes pride in being designed for creators rather than enterprises. Its strength, like Tipeee's, lies in its simplicity. Followers are directed to a page where they can buy as many "coffees" as they want for the creator. In this scenario, "coffees" are $1 contributions sent to the artist via PayPal or online banking.

Ko-fi. Ko-fi provides users with suggestions, subscriptions, and methods to earn commissions for tailored content such as a custom instructional or video chat.

Create a Patreon page and sell fan subscriptions

Crowdfunding works well for large projects, and tipping is the simplest way to gather funds quickly—but what if you want a more consistent source of income? In that situation, you might want to think about adopting a creator-based subscription model like Patreon.

Content creators can make a lot of money with subscription-based income models because they can keep the cost of each subscription low and focus on getting more people to sign up.

A low-cost monthly subscription of, say, one dollar is an easy sell to a single, devoted devotee. When you have a large number of devoted followers, those dollars start to pile up.

Patreon was the first significant platform to allow creators and influencers to generate cash through premium subscriptions from their most devoted followers. You may create membership tiers on Patreon that let you give your most ardent supporters access to unique content.

There are alternatives (most notably Ko-fi, which also incorporates a tipping component), but Patreon offers the added benefit of brand knowledge, which increases trust from prospective supporters.

If you think a subscription service could be the best approach to monetizing your TikTok account, keep the following recommended practices in mind:

- Be open and honest. To be successful on Patreon, you need to earn your supporters' trust by being open and honest about your earnings and expenditures.

- Offer incentives to your fans. Audiences are more likely to raise their donations if they receive something valuable in return. Reward your most ardent supporters with enticing rewards such as unique content and free items.

- Thank donors personally. Make your fans feel valued, and they will be more likely to continue supporting your work. You should try to respond to as many comments as possible, tag users, and offer video shout-outs to as many of your supporters as you can.

- Promote your Patreon account. Fans cannot donate if they are unaware that you are receiving donations. You should include a link to your Patreon page in your TikTok profile and make a note of it in your videos, particularly if you have lately gained a large number of new followers.

- Maintain minimal subscription fees. It is simpler to obtain $1 from 50 followers than $50 from one. Maintain minimal subscription expenses while focusing on increasing your subscriber base.

- Consistently produce new content. When it comes to the frequency with which you produce new content, paying customers have higher expectations. Maintain a content calendar and publish new content on a regular basis.

Go live and earn virtual goodies

One of TikTok's most useful services for creators trying to monetize their content through live streaming is live gifting. Most social networks offer a live streaming capability, but TikTok is unique in that it allows followers to express their gratitude in real-time by giving virtual gifts that may be redeemed for payment.

Here are a few pointers to help you make the most of going live on TikTok:

- Choose the best moment. You should go live when the majority of your audience is online. Go to your profile settings and click the Analytics tab to observe when your audience is most active.

- Continue to live longer. You may not get the full attention of everyone who watches your live stream, but if you stay online for a longer period of time, more people will have an opportunity to see it.

- During your live stream, make a post. When you submit a short video while you are live on TikTok, people who see the video in their stream are prompted with a link to your live broadcast. This helps build your following while you are live.

- Make use of TikTok hashtags. Users, like those on other social media platforms, routinely explore hashtag sites in search of new accounts to follow. To improve the reach of your videos, use TikTok's hashtags.

- Check your equipment, including your internet connection. Don't forget to consider the technical implications of going live. Make sure your lighting, sound, and internet connections can all be used for extended periods of time.

- Keep yourself safe. Keep in mind that TikTok allows you to block viewers, mute users, and filter comments. Don't be hesitant to utilize these features on users who aren't contributing in good faith to the conversation. Nobody should be subjected to bullying or harassment.

Real-time interaction with users is a terrific way to establish lasting bonds with your followers. Going live can also assist in increasing other monetization streams because audiences that have a deep connection to a creator often take an interest in their success personally.

You can advertise your products on Tiktok

If you already have items, this is the most apparent way to generate money: make TikToks that showcase your products, including all of the features that make them special. Make sure your bio includes a link to your shop.

TikTok has a plethora of excellent organic marketing opportunities, but if you're prepared to pay a little money to increase the reach of your content, you should consider designing your own in-feed advertising using the TikTok ads manager.

TikTok adverts display in viewers' "For you" feed and play automatically, just like any other TikTok video. You may ensure that your videos reach the viewers who are most interested in your products by using paid adverts.

But the best thing is... TikTok's ad manager works in tandem with Shopify. That means you can create TikTok advertisements, choose a target audience, and track the performance of your ads all from your Shopify store.

Take part in Affiliate Programs

TikTok does not require you to have your own products or services to gain money. Instead, utilize affiliate marketing to link to other products and earn a share of each transaction when a user clicks through and buys. Here's how it's done:

- Put an affiliate link in your profile and divert traffic from organic views to it.
- You should reroute traffic to your Facebook, Twitter, or Pinterest account since this will allow you to post affiliate links in a more generous manner.
- In your video captions, including promo codes and URLs. Users must copy and paste the link into their browser.

Promote Songs

You can get paid to promote songs if you add them to your videos. Nearly every TikTok video has a song in the background that creators can lip-sync and dance to, and artists know how important this is. Musicians will pay you to advertise their music in your songs if you have a large enough audience and interaction.

They understand that if your video goes viral, so will their song, which means more downloads, concert tickets, and merchandise.

TikTok can help you advertise your music if you're a musician (or wannabe musician). TikTok is a platform for singing and dancing; therefore, it only makes sense to upload your own beats.

Create and sell TikTok accounts

Do you have a talent for fast-growing an audience? Make a living from it.

There are a lot of people and businesses who would want to get a head start on TikTok. You'll have a list of possible buyers if you can quickly create TikTok followings.

Consider prospective sectors that might be interested in purchasing a successful TikTok account. An account focused on cat GIFs may struggle to sell (or may not), but an unboxing profile or account focused on vehicles will most likely sell considerably faster.

Don't personalize these accounts. You don't want your name or face to become associated with your followers. Instead, you should concentrate your information on the topic at hand.

Made in United States
Troutdale, OR
01/08/2024

16809931R00051